TOSEL®

JUNIOR

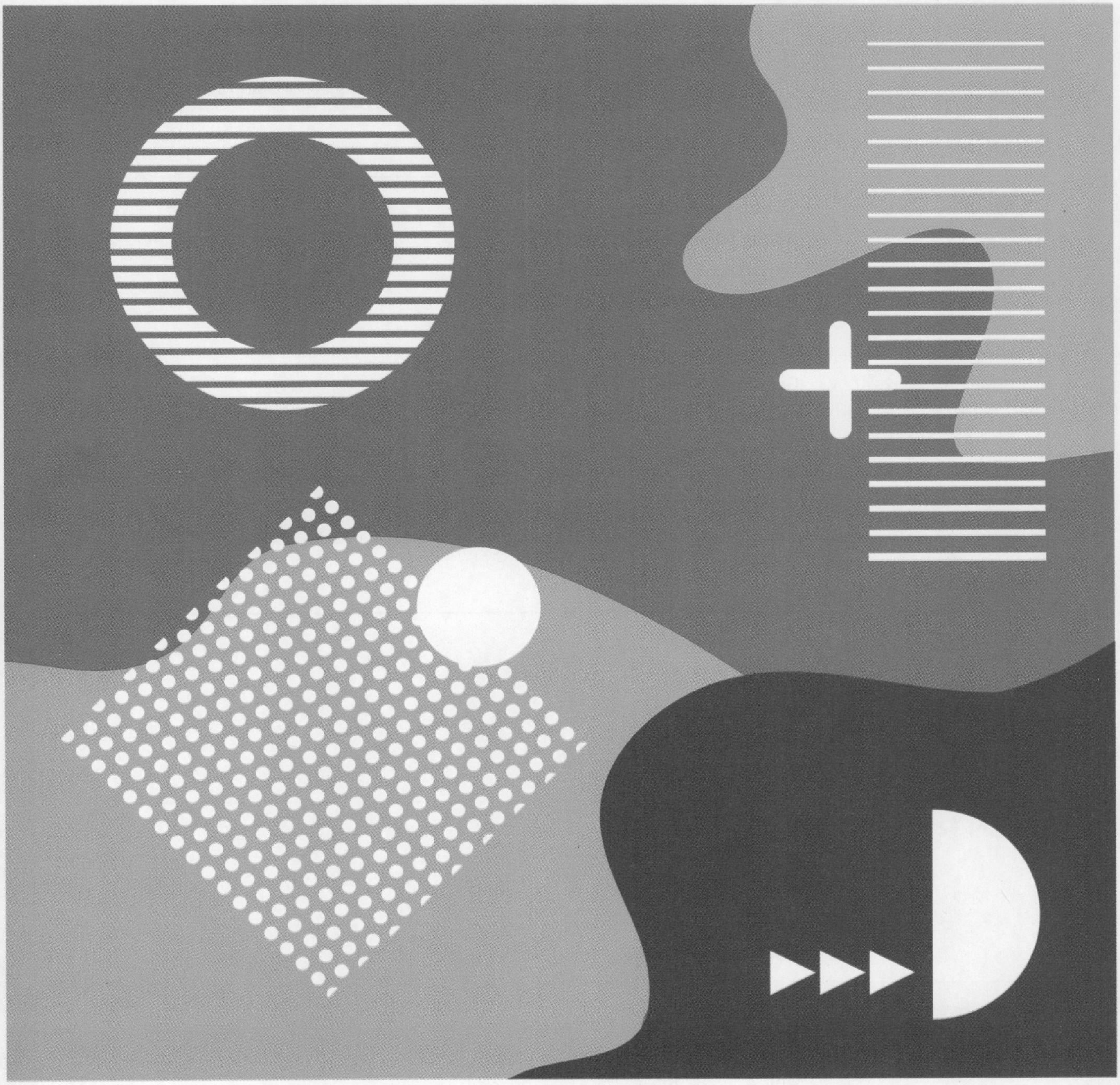

GRAMMAR 1

International TOSEL Committee

CONTENTS

BROCHURES

Junior 1권

Junior 2권

TOSEL® Level Chart TOSEL 단계표

COCOON

아이들이 접할 수 있는 공식 인증 시험의 첫 단계로써, 아이들의 부담을 줄이고 즐겁게 흥미를 유발할 수 있도록 컬러풀한 색상과 디자인으로 시험지를 구성하였습니다.

Pre-STARTER

친숙한 주제에 대한 단어, 짧은 대화, 짧은 문장을 사용한 기본적인 문장표현 능력을 측정합니다.

STARTER

흔히 접할 수 있는 주제와 상황과 관련된 주제에 대한 짧은 대화 및 짧은 문장을 이해하고 일상생활 대화에 참여하며 실질적인 영어 기초 의사소통 능력을 측정합니다.

BASIC

개인 정보와 일상 활동, 미래 계획, 과거의 경험에 대해 구어와 문어의 형태로 의사소통을 할 수 있는 능력을 측정합니다.

JUNIOR

일반적인 주제와 상황을 다루는 회화와 짧은 단락, 실용문, 짧은 연설 등을 이해하고 간단한 일상 대화에 참여하는 능력을 측정합니다.

HIGH JUNIOR

넓은 범위의 사회적, 학문적 주제에서 영어를 유창하고 정확하게, 효과적으로 사용할 수 있는 능력 및 중문과 복잡한 문장을 포함한 다양한 문장구조의 사용 능력을 측정합니다.

ADVANCED

대학 및 대학원에서 요구되는 영어능력과 취업 또는 직업근무환경에 필요한 실용영어 능력을 측정합니다.

TOSEL
교재 Series

교과 과정 및 교재별 연계

TOSEL LEVEL	Age	Vocabulary Frequency	Readability Score	교과 과정 연계	Grammar	VOCA	Reading	Listening
Cocoon	K5-K7	500	0-1	Who is he? (국어 1단원 1-1)	There is · There are	150	Picking Pumpkins (Phonics Story)	Phonics
Pre-Starter	P1-P2	700	1-2	How old are you? (통합교과 1-1)	be + adjective	300	Me & My Family (Reading series Ch.1)	묘사하기
Starter	P3-P4	1000-2000		Spring, Summer, Fall, Winter (통합교과 3-1)	Simple Present	800	Ask More Questions (Reading Series Ch.1)	날씨/시간 표현
Basic	P5-P6	3000-4000	3-4	Show and Tell (사회 5-1)	Superlative	1700	Culture (Reading Series Ch.3)	상대방 의견 묻고 답하기
Junior	M1-M2	5000-6000	5-6	중 1, 2 과학, 기술가정	to-infinitive	4000	Humans and Animals (Reading Series Ch.1)	정보 묻고 답하기
High Junior	H1-H3			고등학교 - 체육	2nd Conditional	7000	Health (Reading Series Ch.1)	사건 묘사하기

■ TOSEL의 세분화된 레벨은 각 연령에 맞는 어휘와 읽기 지능 및 교과 과정과의 연계가 가능하도록 설계된 교재들로 효과적인 학습 커리큘럼을 제공합니다.

■ TOSEL의 커리큘럼에 따른 학습은

정확한 레벨링 → 레벨에 적합한 학습 → 영어 능력 인증 시험 TOSEL에서의 공신력 있는 평가를 통해 진단 → 학습 → 평가의 선순환 구조를 실현합니다.

About TOSEL® — TOSEL에 대하여

TOSEL은 각급 학교 교과과정과 연령별 인지단계를 고려하여 단계별 난이도와 문항으로
영어 숙달 정도를 측정하는 영어 사용자 중심의 맞춤식 영어능력인증 시험제도입니다.
평가유형에 따른 개인별 장점과 단점을 파악하고, 개인별 영어학습 방향을 제시하는 성적분석자료를 제공하여
영어능력 종합검진 서비스를 제공함으로써 영어 사용자인 소비자와
영어능력 평가를 토대로 영어교육을 담당하는 교사 및 기관 인사관리자인 공급자를
모두 만족시키는 영어능력인증 평가입니다.

TOSEL은 인지적-학문적 언어 사용의 유창성 (Cognitive-Academic Language Proficiency, CALP)과
기본적-개인적 의사소통능력 (Basic Interpersonal Communication Skill, BICS)을
엄밀히 구분하여 수험자의 언어능력을 가장 친밀하게 평가하는 시험입니다.

대상	목적	용도
유아, 초, 중, 고등학생, 대학생 및 직장인 등 성인	한국인의 영어구사능력 증진과 비영어권 국가의 영어 사용자의 영어구사능력 증진	실질적인 영어구사능력 평가 + 입학전형 및 인재선발 등에 활용 및 직무역량별 인재 배치

연혁

2002.02	국제토셀위원회 창설 (수능출제위원역임 전국대학 영어전공교수진 중심)
2004.09	TOSEL 고려대학교 국제어학원 공동인증시험 실시
2006.04	EBS 한국교육방송공사 주관기관 참여
2006.05	민족사관고등학교 입학전형에 반영
2008.12	고려대학교 편입학시험 TOSEL 유형으로 대체
2009.01	서울시 공무원 근무평정에 TOSEL 점수 가산점 부여
2009.01	전국 대부분 외고, 자사고 입학전형에 TOSEL 반영 (한영외국어고등학교, 한일고등학교, 고양외국어고등학교, 과천외국어고등학교, 김포외국어고등학교, 명지외국어고등학교, 부산국제외국어고등학교, 부일외국어 고등학교, 성남외국어고등학교, 인천외국어고등학교, 전북외국어고등학교, 대전외국어고등학교, 청주외국어고등학교, 강원외국어고등학교, 전남외국어고등학교)
2009.12	청심국제중 • 고등학교 입학전형 TOSEL 반영
2009.12	한국외국어교육학회, 팬코리아영어교육학회, 한국음성학회, 한국응용언어학회 TOSEL 인증
2010.03	고려대학교, TOSEL 출제기관 및 공동 인증기관으로 참여
2010.07	경찰청 공무원 임용 TOSEL 성적 가산점 부여
2014.04	전국 200개 초등학교 단체 응시 실시
2017.03	중앙일보 주관기관 참여
2018.11	관공서, 대기업 등 100여 개 기관에서 TOSEL 반영
2019.06	미얀마 TOSEL 도입 발족식 베트남 TOSEL 도입 협약식
2019.11	2020학년도 고려대학교 편입학전형 반영
2020.04	국토교통부 국가자격시험 TOSEL 반영
2021.07	소방청 간부후보생 선발시험 TOSEL 반영

About TOSEL® — TOSEL에 대하여

What's TOSEL?

"Test of Skills in the English Language"

TOSEL은 비영어권 국가의 영어 사용자를 대상으로 영어구사능력을 측정하여 그 결과를 공식 인증하는 영어능력인증 시험제도입니다.

영어 사용자 중심의 맞춤식 영어능력 인증 시험제도

맞춤식 평가

획일적인 평가에서 세분화된 평가로의 전환

TOSEL은 응시자의 연령별 인지단계에 따라 별도의 문항과 난이도를 적용하여 평가함으로써 평가의 목적과 용도에 적합한 평가 시스템을 구축하였습니다.

공정성과 신뢰성 확보

국제토셀위원회의 역할

TOSEL은 고려대학교가 출제 및 인증기관으로 참여하였고 대학입학수학능력시험 출제위원 교수들이 중심이 된 국제토셀위원회가 주관하여 사회적 공정성과 신뢰성을 확보한 평가 제도입니다.

수입대체 효과

외화유출 차단 및 국위선양

TOSEL은 해외시험응시로 인한 외화의 유출을 막는 수입대체의 효과를 기대할 수 있습니다. TOSEL의 문항과 시험제도는 비영어권 국가에 수출하여 국위선양에 기여하고 있습니다.

Why TOSEL® — 왜 TOSEL인가

01 학교 시험 폐지

일선 학교에서 중간, 기말고사 폐지로 인해 객관적인 영어 평가 제도의 부재가 우려됩니다. 그러나 전국단위로 연간 4번 시행되는 TOSEL 평가시험을 통해 학생들은 정확한 역량과 체계적인 학습방향을 꾸준히 진단받을 수 있습니다.

02 연령별/단계별 대비로 영어학습 점검

TOSEL은 응시자의 연령별 인지단계 및 영어 학습 단계에 따라 총 7단계로 구성되었습니다. 각 단계에 알맞은 문항유형과 난이도를 적용해 모든 연령 및 학습 과정에 맞추어 가장 효율적으로 영어실력을 평가할 수 있도록 개발된 영어시험입니다.

03 학교내신성적 향상

TOSEL은 학년별 교과과정과 연계하여 학교에서 배우는 내용을 학습하고 평가할 수 있도록 문항 및 주제를 구성하여 내신영어 향상을 위한 최적의 솔루션을 제공합니다.

04 수능대비 직결

유아, 초, 중등시절 어렵지 않고 즐겁게 학습해 온 영어이지만, 수능시험준비를 위해 접하는 영어의 문항 및 유형 난이도에 주춤하게 됩니다. 이를 대비하기 위해 TOSEL은 유아부터 성인까지 점진적인 학습을 통해 수능대비를 자연적으로 해나갈 수 있습니다.

05 진학과 취업에 대비한 필수 스펙관리

개인별 '학업성취기록부' 발급을 통해 영어학업성취이력을 꾸준히 기록한 영어학습 포트폴리오를 제공하여 영어학습 이력을 관리할 수 있습니다.

06 자기소개서에 토셀 기재

개별적인 진로 적성 Report를 제공하여 진로를 파악하고 자기소개서 작성시 적극적으로 활용할 수 있는 객관적인 자료를 제공합니다.

07 영어학습 동기부여

시험실시 후 응시자 모두에게 수여되는 인증서는 영어학습에 대한 자신감과 성취감을 고취시키고 동기를 부여합니다.

08 AI 분석 영어학습 솔루션

국내외 15,000여 개 학교·학원 단체 응시인원 중 엄선한 100만 명 이상의 실제 TOSEL 성적 데이터를 기반으로 영어인증시험 제도 중 세계 최초로 인공지능이 분석한 개인별 AI 정밀 진단 성적표를 제공합니다. 최첨단 AI 정밀진단 성적표는 최적의 영어 학습 솔루션을 제시하여 영어 학습에 소요되는 시간과 노력을 획기적으로 절감해줍니다.

09 명예의 전당, 우수협력기관 지정

우수교육기관은 'TOSEL 우수 협력 기관'에 지정되고, 각 시/도별, 최고득점자를 명예의 전당에 등재합니다.

Evaluation — 평가

평가의 기본원칙

TOSEL은 PBT(Paper Based Test)를 통하여 간접평가와 직접평가를 모두 시행합니다.

TOSEL은 언어의 네 가지 요소인 **읽기, 듣기, 말하기, 쓰기 영역을 모두 평가합니다.**

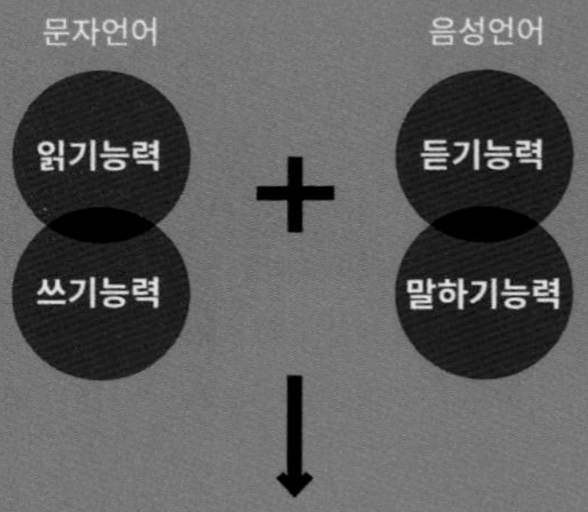

대한민국 대표 영어능력 인증 시험제도

TOSEL®

Reading 읽기	모든 레벨의 읽기 영역은 직접 평가 방식으로 측정합니다.
Listening 듣기	모든 레벨의 듣기 영역은 직접 평가 방식으로 측정합니다.
Writing 쓰기	모든 레벨의 쓰기 영역은 간접 평가 방식으로 측정합니다.
Speaking 말하기	모든 레벨의 말하기 영역은 간접 평가 방식으로 측정합니다.

TOSEL은 연령별 인지단계를 고려하여 **아래와 같이 7단계로 나누어 평가합니다.**

1 단계	TOSEL® COCOON	**5~7세의 미취학 아동**
2 단계	TOSEL® Pre-STARTER	**초등학교 1~2학년**
3 단계	TOSEL® STARTER	**초등학교 3~4학년**
4 단계	TOSEL® BASIC	**초등학교 5~6학년**
5 단계	TOSEL® JUNIOR	**중학생**
6 단계	TOSEL® HIGH JUNIOR	**고등학생**
7 단계	TOSEL® ADVANCED	**대학생 및 성인**

Grade Report — 성적표 및 인증서

개인 AI 정밀진단 성적표

십 수년간 전국단위 정기시험으로 축적된 빅데이터를 교육공학적으로 분석 · 활용하여 산출한 개인별 성적자료

정확한 영어능력진단 / 섹션별 · 파트별 영어능력 및 균형 진단 / 명예의 전당 등재 여부 / 온라인 최적화된 개인별 상세 성적자료를 위한 QR코드 / 응시지역, 동일학년, 전국에서의 학생의 위치

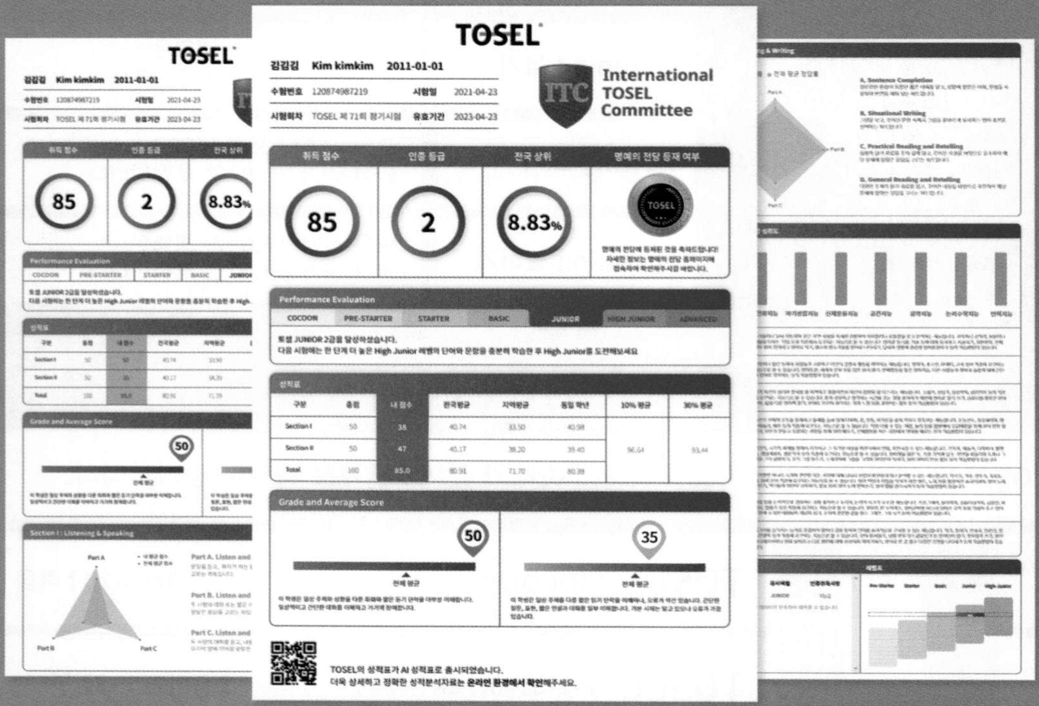

단체 및 기관 응시자 AI 통계 분석 자료

십 수년간 전국단위 정기시험으로 **축적된 빅데이터를 교육공학적으로 분석 · 활용**하여 산출한 응시자 통계 분석 자료

- 단체 내 레벨별 평균성적추이, LR평균 점수, 표준편차 파악
- 타 지역 내 다른 단체와의 점수 종합 비교 / 단체 내 레벨별 학생분포 파악
- 동일 지역 내 다른 단체 레벨별 응시자의 평균 나이 비교
- 동일 지역 내 다른 단체 명예의 전당 등재 인원 수 비교
- 동일 지역 내 다른 단체 최고점자의 최고 점수 비교
- 동일 지역 내 다른 응시자들의 수 비교

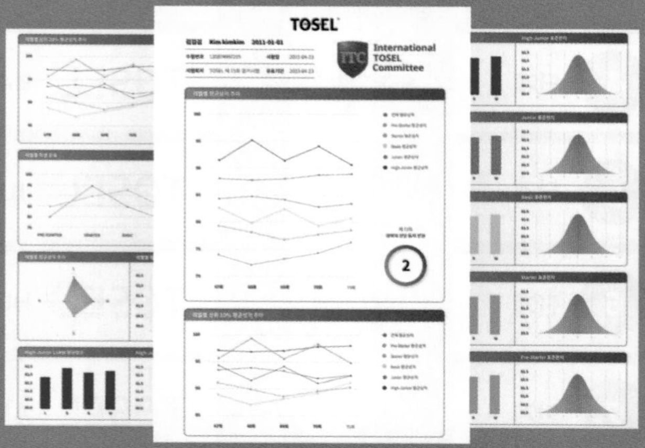

'토셀 명예의 전당' 등재

특별시, 광역시, 도 별 **1등 선발**
(7개시 9개도 **1등 선발**)

*홈페이지 로그인 - 시험결과 - 명예의 전당에서
해당자 등재 증명서 출력 가능

'학업성취기록부'에 토셀 인증등급 기재

개인별 **'학업성취기록부' 평생 발급**
진학과 취업을 대비한 **필수 스펙관리**

인증서

대한민국 초,중,고등학생의 영어숙달능력 평가 결과 공식인증

고려대학교 인증획득 (2010. 03) 팬코리아영어교육학회 인증획득 (2009. 10) 한국응용언어학회 인증획득 (2009. 11)
한국외국어교육학회 인증획득 (2009. 12) 한국음성학회 인증획득 (2009. 12)

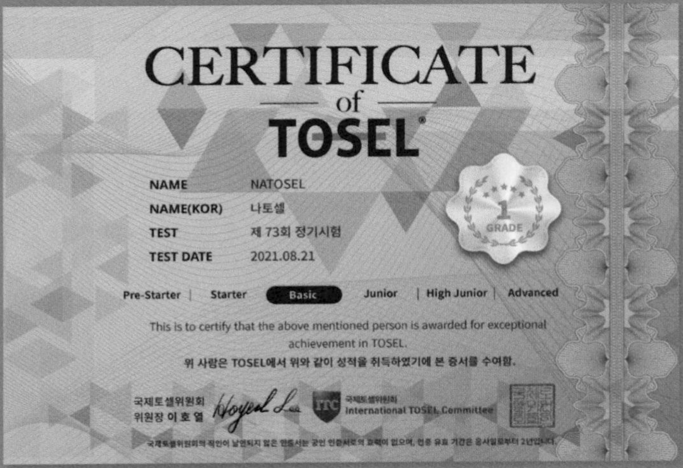

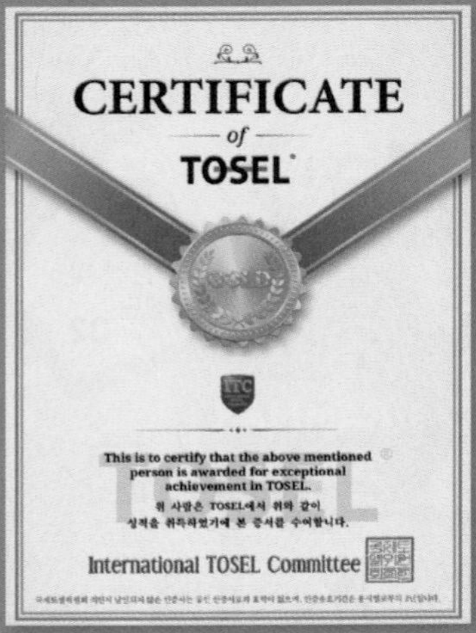

Grammar Series ——— 특장점

TOSEL 시험을 기준으로 빈출 지표를 활용한 문법 선정 및 예문과 문제 구성

TOSEL 시험 활용

- 실제 TOSEL 시험에 출제된 빈출 문항을 기준으로 단계별 학습을 위한 문법 선정
- 실제 TOSEL 시험에 활용된 문장을 사용하여 예문과 문제를 구성
- 문법 학습 이외에 TOSEL 기출 문제 풀이를 통해서 TOSEL 및 실전 영어 시험 대비 학습

세분화된 레벨링

20년 간 대한민국 영어 평가 기관으로서
연간 4회 전국적으로 실시되는 정기시험에서
축적된 성적 데이터를 기반으로
정확하고 세분화된 레벨링을 통한
영어 학습 콘텐츠 개발

언어의 4대 영역 균형 학습 + 평가

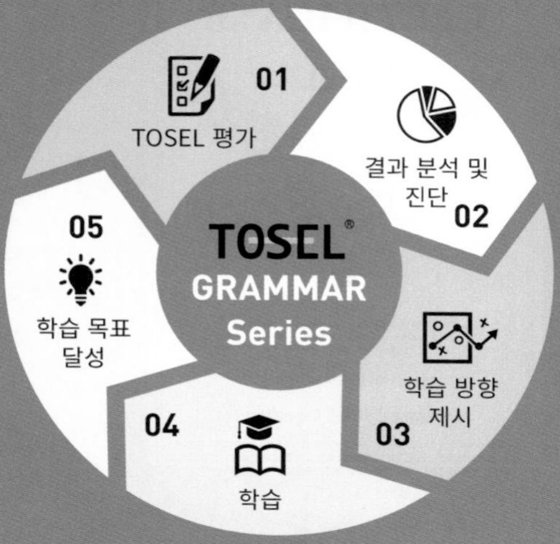

1 TOSEL 평가: 학생의 영어 능력을 정확하게 평가

2 결과 분석 및 진단: 시험 점수와 결과를 분석하여 학생의 강점, 취약점, 학습자 특성 등을 객관적으로 진단

3 학습 방향 제시: 객관적 진단 데이터를 기반으로 학습자 특성에 맞는 학습 방향 제시 및 목표 설정

4 학습: 제시된 방향과 목표에 따라 학생에게 적합한 문법 학습법 소개 및 영어의 체계와 구조 이해

5 학습 목표 달성: 학습 후 다시 평가를 통해 목표 달성 여부 확인 및 성장을 위한 다음 학습 목표 설정

Grammar Series

LEVEL

TOSEL의 Grammar Series는 레벨에 맞게 단계적으로
문법을 학습할 수 있도록 구성되어 있습니다.

Pre-Starter | Starter | Basic | Junior | High Junior

- 그림을 활용하여 문법에 대한 이해도 향상
- 다양한 활동을 통해 문법 반복 학습 유도
- TOSEL 기출 문제 연습을 통한 실전 대비

- TOSEL 기출의 빈도수를 활용한 문법 선정으로 효율적 학습
- 실제 TOSEL 지문의 예문을 활용한 실용적 학습 제공
- TOSEL 기출 문제 연습을 통한 실전 대비

최신 수능 출제
문법을 포함하여
수능 대비 가능

70분 학습 Guideline

01 Unit Intro

2분

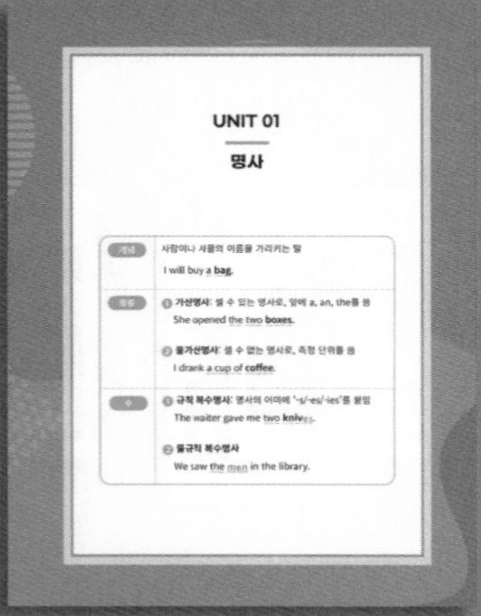

■ 중등 교육과정에서 익혀야 하는 문법과 단어를 중심으로 단원의 문법에 대해 미리 생각해보기

02 개념

15분

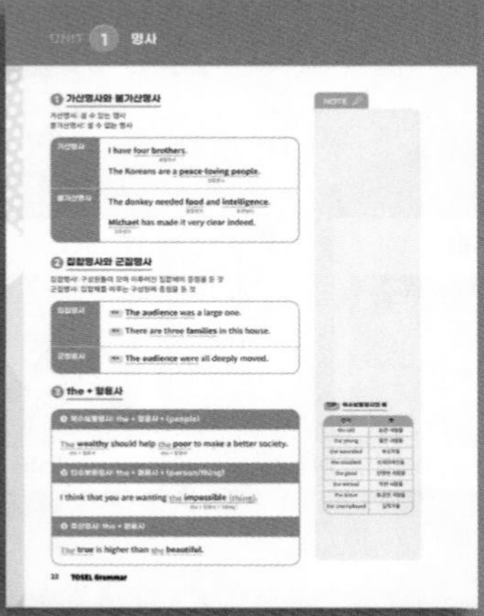

■ Unit Intro의 요약을 표로 구조화하여 세부적으로 학습하기 용이하게 구성

05 Sentence Completion

10분

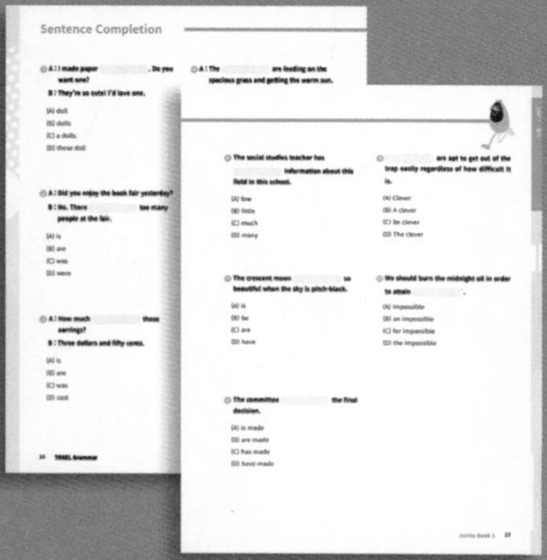

■ Unit에서 배운 문법을 활용하여 문제 해결하기

■ 빈칸 채우기, 알맞은 표현 고르기 등 TOSEL 실전 문제 학습

■ 틀린 문제에 대해서는 해당 Unit에서 복습하도록 지도하기

06 Error Recognition

10분

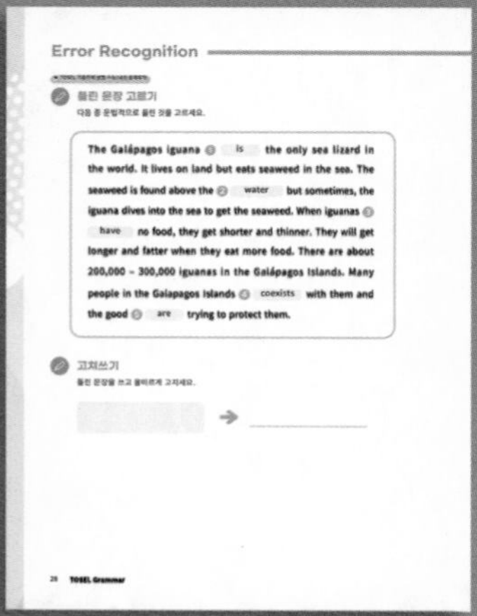

■ 수능 유형의 실전 문제 학습을 통해 TOSEL 시험 뿐만 아니라 수능 영어 또한 대비 가능

■ 5개년 TOSEL 기출을 활용하여 더욱 생생한 문법

03 Activity

3분

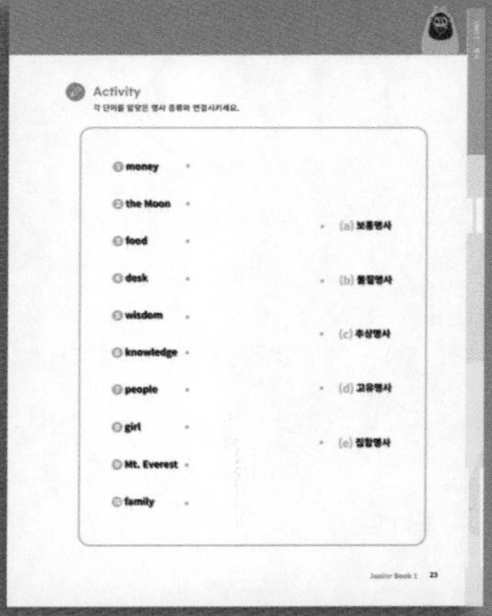
Activity
money
the Moon
food
desk
wisdom
knowledge
people
girl
Mt. Everest
family
(a) 보통명사
(b) 물질명사
(c) 추상명사
(d) 고유명사
(e) 집합명사

- 배운 문법을 활용하여 문제 해결하기
- Matching, O/X 활동을 하며 문법의 기초 학습

04 Exercise

10분

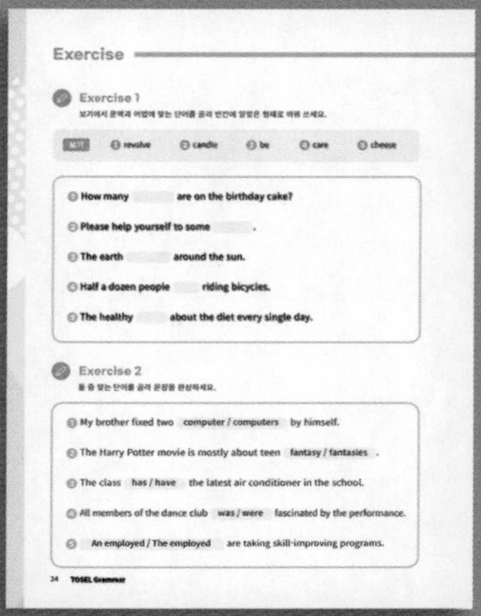
Exercise
Exercise 1
revolve candle be care cheese
How many ______ are on the birthday cake?
Please help yourself to some ______.
The earth ______ around the sun.
Half a dozen people ______ riding bicycles.
The healthy ______ about the diet every single day.
Exercise 2
My brother fixed two computer / computers by himself.
The Harry Potter movie is mostly about teen fantasy / fantasies.
The class has / have the latest air conditioner in the school.
All members of the dance club was / were fascinated by the performance.
An employed / The employed are taking skill-improving programs.

- 다양한 Exercise 활동을 하며 혼동하기 쉬운 문법 학습
- 문장 안에 문법적으로 알맞은 단어를 선택하거나 쓰는 활동을 하며 혼동하기 쉬운 문법 학습

07 Unit Review

10분

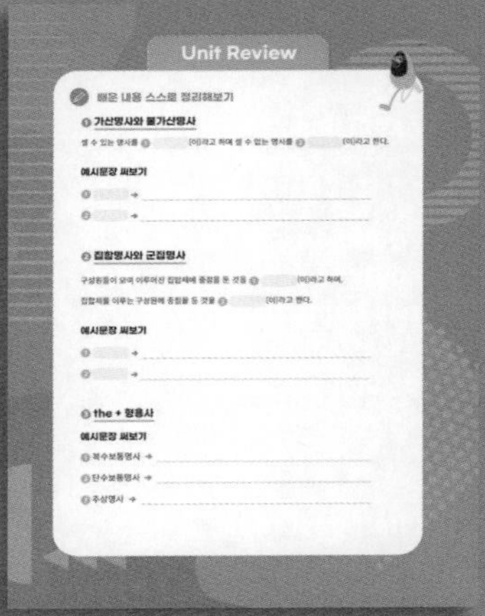
Unit Review

- 빈칸을 채우는 형태로 구성하여 수업 시간 후 복습에 용이하게 구성
- 배운 문법을 활용하여 예시 문장을 직접 써보는 시간

08 TOSEL 실전문제

10분

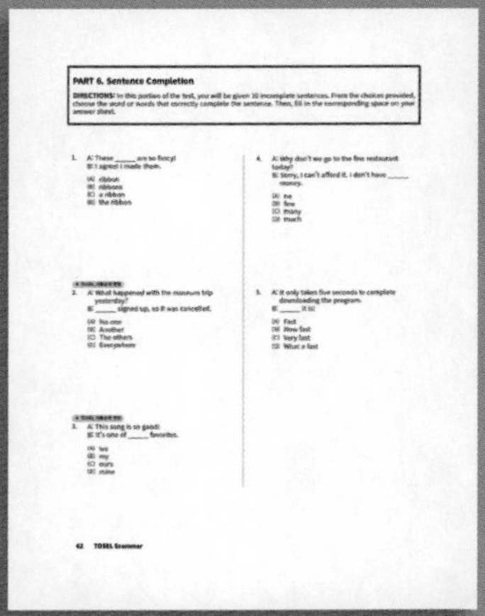
PART 6. Sentence Completion

- 실제 TOSEL 기출 문제를 통한 실전 대비 학습
- 실제 시험 시간과 유사하게 풀이할 수 있도록 지도하기
- 틀린 문제에 대해서는 해당 단원에서 복습하도록 지도하기

PreStarter/Starter/Basic
Syllabus

PreStarter		Basic		2015 개정 초등 영어 언어형식
Chapter	Unit	Chapter	Unit	
I. 명사: 명사는 이름이야	1 셀 수 있는 명사	**I. 명사**	1 셀 수 있는 명사 앞에 붙는 관사 the/a/an	**A** boy/The **boy**/The (two) boys ran in the park. **The** store is closed.
	2 셀 수 있는 명사 앞에 붙는 관사 a/an		2 셀 수 없는 명사를 측정하는 단위	**Water** is very important for life. **Kate** is from **London**.
	3 셀 수 없는 명사		3 규칙 복수명사	The **two boys** ran in the park.
	4 명사의 복수형		4 불규칙 복수명사	
II. 대명사: 명사를 대신하는 대명사	1 주격 대명사	**II. 대명사**	1 단수대명사의 격	**She** is a teacher, and **he**'s a scientist. I like **your** glasses. What about **mine**?
	2 소유격 대명사		2 복수대명사의 격	**They**'re really delicious. **We** are very glad to hear from him.
	3 목적격 대명사		3 1, 2인칭 대명사의 활용	**I** like math, but Susan doesn't like it. He will help **you**.
	4 지시대명사		4 3인칭 대명사의 활용	Which do you like better, **this** or **that**? **These** are apples, and **those** are tomatoes. **That** dog is smart. **These/Those** books are really large.
III. 형용사: 명사&대명사를 꾸미는 형용사	1 형용사의 명사수식	**III. 동사**	1 동사의 기본시제	He **walks** to school every day. We **played** soccer yesterday. She **is going to** visit her grandparents next week. He **is sleeping** now. I **will visit** America next year.
	2 형용사의 대명사수식		2 동사의 불규칙 과거형	
	3 숫자와 시간		3 헷갈리기 쉬운 동사	**It's half past four.** **What time** is it? I **don't** like snakes. We **didn't** enjoy the movie very much.
	4 지시형용사		4 조동사	She **can** play the violin. Tom **won't** be at the meeting tomorrow. I **will** visit America next year. You **may** leave now.

Starter		Basic		2015 개정 초등 영어 언어형식
Chapter	**Unit**	**Chapter**	**Unit**	
I. 동사: 동사는 움직임이야	1 be동사	**IV. 형용사와 부사**	1 형용사 vs. 부사	**Many** young people have no money. We didn't buy **much/any** food. **Every** monkey likes bananas. **All** children love baby animals.
	2 의문사+be동사		2 수량형용사	
	3 3인칭 단수동사		3 빈도부사	We **usually** meet after lunch.
	4 동사의 현재시제		4 비교급과 최상급	Mary is **taller than I/me**.
II. 부사: 동사를 꾸미는 부사	1 일반적인 부사의 생김새	**V. 접속사와 전치사**	1 단어를 연결하는 접속사	John **and** Mary are good friends. They are my neighbors, **but** I don't know them well.
	2 예외적인 부사의 생김새		2 문장을 연결하는 접속사	He went to bed **because** he was sleepy.
	3 부사와 형용사의 비교		3 시간과 장소를 나타내는 전치사	There are two books **on** the desk.
	4 부사와 문장의 배열		4 그 밖의 전치사	
III. 전치사: 시간, 장소, 위치, 방향을 나타내는 전치사	1 시간을 나타내는 전치사	**VI. 문장**	1 문장의 형식	The baby **cried**. You **look happy** today. He **is a match teacher**. I **like gimbap**.
	2 장소를 나타내는 전치사		2 명령문	**Open** your book. **Let's go** to Brian's birthday party.
	3 위치를 나타내는 전치사		3 의문문	**Are you** ready? **Does** Anne work out on weekends?
	4 방향을 나타내는 전치사		4 부가의문문	**Why** did he leave early? **How** do you spell your name? **Who** can answer that question? **Whose dolls** are these? **What time** is it?

Junior Syllabus

Junior		2015 개정 중등 영어 언어형식
Chapter	**Unit**	
I. 8품사 (1)	1 명사	She lived in the **woods** when she was kid. Thank you for your **kindness**.
	2 대명사	I have **three books**. **One** is mine. **The others** are yours. **The chocolate cookie** is sweet. I'm going to have **another one**.
	3 형용사	Something **strange** happened last night.
	4 감탄사	**How** beautiful she is! **What** a player!
II 8품사 (2)	1 동사	**Mathematics** is my favorite subject. **Each** boy admires his teacher. **Both** the teacher **and** the students enjoyed the class. You can have **either** tea or coffee. It is **not only** beautiful **but (also)** useful.
	2 부사	
	3 전치사	
	4 접속사	I may stop by tomorrow **or** just phone you. Both the teacher **and** the students enjoyed the class.
III. 문장의 구조	1 문장성분의 기초	You can **put the dish on the table**. He **gave me a present**. They **elected him president**.
	2 문장의 형식	
	3 평서문의 전환	
	4 의문문의 비교	**Have you** finished your homework yet? This is your book, **isn't it**?
IV. 문장의 시제	1 단순시제	I **will be** able to help you get to the party tonight. **Are you going** to take the last train?
	2 진행시제	I**'m thinking** about the problem. I **was studying** when John called me.
	3 현재완료	The bakery **has been** open since 1960. He **has attended** the club meetings regularly.
	4 시간을 나타내는 접속사	**Since** he left this morning, I haven't seen him. **When** we arrived, she was talking on the phone.
V. to부정사와 동명사	1 to부정사	**To see** is **to belive**. Chris was glad **to hear the news**.
	2 동명사	We **enjoy swimming** in the pool. Life is **worth living**. I'm interested in **watching horror movies**.
	3 to부정사와 동명사 비교	
	4 의미상주어	It is difficult **for me to speak French**. It was kind **of you to help us**.
VI. 비교급과 최상급	1 비교급과 최상급의 규칙 변화	They've got **more/less** money **than** they need. A car is **much more** expensive **than** a motorbike.
	2 비교급과 최상급의 불규칙 변화	
	3 원급의 비교	You can run **as fast as** Billy can. She is old, but she is not **as old as** he (is).
	4 최상급의 비교	Cindy is **the shortest** of the three. It is **the most interesting** speech I've ever heard.

High Junior Syllabus

High Junior		2015 개정 중등 영어 언어형식
Chapter	Unit	
I. 문장의 형성	1 8품사와 문장 성분 2 문장의 형식	**The audience** is/are enjoying the show. I'd like to **write a diary**, but I'm too busy to do so. He**'s being** very rude. We **are hoping** you will be with us.
	3 문장의 배열	I think **(that)** he is a good actor. **Although/Though** it was cold, I went swimming.
	4 문장의 강조	The weather was **so** nice **that** we went hiking. **It was Justin who/that** told me the truth.
II 부정사와 동명사	1 원형부정사	You shouldn't **let** him **go** there again. I **heard** the children **sing/singing**.
	2 to부정사 3 동명사 4 to부정사와 동명사구	He seemed **to have been ill (for some time)**. Bill promised Jane **to work out with her**. I remembered **John/John's coming late for class**. It goes without **saying that time is money**. There is no use **crying over the spilt milk**.
III. 분사	1 현재분사	At the station I met a lady **carrying a large umbrella**. **With the night coming**, stars began to shine in the sky.
	2 과거분사	Wallets **found on the street** must be reported to the police.
	3 분사구문	**Walking along the street,** I met an old friend. **Having seen that movie before,** I wanted to see it again.
	4 독립분사구문	**Joshua returning home,** the puppy ran toward him. **Frankly speaking,** I failed the test.
IV. 수동태	1 수동태의 형성 2 수동태와 능동태의 전환 3 수동태와 전치사의 사용 4 주의해야 할 수동태 용법	The building **was built** in 1880. I **was made** to clean the room. Nolan **was seen** to enter the building. The monkey **has been raised** by human parents for years. Cooper **will be invited** to today's meeting. The information superhighway **will have been introduced** to everyone by 2015.
V. 관계대명사와 관계부사	1 관계대명사의 사용	The girl **who is playing the piano** is called Ann. This is the book **(that) I bought yesterday**.
	2 관계대명사와 선행사	Please tell me **what happened**.
	3 관계대명사의 생략	This is **why** we have to study English grammar.
	4 관계부사	The town **in which I was born** is very small. That's just **how he talks**, always serious about his work.
VI. 가정법	1 가정법 현재와 과거	**If it were not for you,** I **would** be lonely.
	2 가정법 과거완료	**Had** I had enough money, I **would have bought** a cell phone. **Without/But for** your advice, I **would have** failed.
	3 혼합가정법 4 특수가정법	I **wish** I **had learned** swimming last summer. He acts **as if** he **had been** there. I'd **rather** we **had** dinner now. **Provided that/As long as** they had plenty to eat, the crew **seemed** to be happy.

CHAPTER 01

I. 8품사 (1)

UNIT 01

명사

개념	사람이나 사물의 이름을 가리키는 말 I will buy a **bag**.
종류	❶ **가산명사**: 셀 수 있는 명사로, 앞에 a, an, the를 씀 She opened the two **boxes**. ❷ **불가산명사**: 셀 수 없는 명사로, 측정 단위를 씀 I drank a cup of **coffee**.
수	❶ **규칙 복수명사**: 명사의 어미에 '-s/-es/-ies'를 붙임 The waiter gave me two **knives**. ❷ **불규칙 복수명사** We saw the **men** in the library.

UNIT 1 명사

① 가산명사와 불가산명사

가산명사: 셀 수 있는 명사
불가산명사: 셀 수 없는 명사

가산명사	I have four brothers. (brothers: 보통명사) The Koreans are a peace-loving people. (people: 집합명사)
불가산명사	The donkey needed food and intelligence. (food: 물질명사, intelligence: 추상명사) Michael has made it very clear indeed. (Michael: 고유명사)

② 집합명사와 군집명사

집합명사: 구성원들이 모여 이루어진 집합체에 중점을 둔 것
군집명사: 집합체를 이루는 구성원에 중점을 둔 것

집합명사	단수 The audience was a large one. 복수 There are three families in this house.
군집명사	복수 The audience were all deeply moved.

③ the + 형용사

① 복수보통명사: the + 형용사 + (people)

The wealthy should help the poor to make a better society.
(The wealthy: the + 형용사, the poor: the + 형용사)

② 단수보통명사: the + 형용사 + (person/thing)

I think that you are wanting the impossible (thing).
(the impossible (thing): the + 형용사 + (thing))

③ 추상명사: the + 형용사

The true is higher than the beautiful.

NOTE

TIP 복수보통명사의 예

단어	뜻
the old	늙은 사람들
the young	젊은 사람들
the wounded	부상자들
the disabled	신체장애인들
the good	선량한 사람들
the wicked	악한 사람들
the brave	용감한 사람들
the unemployed	실직자들

Activity

각 단어를 알맞은 명사 종류와 연결시키세요.

❶ money •
❷ the Moon •
❸ food •
❹ desk •
❺ wisdom •
❻ knowledge •
❼ people •
❽ girl •
❾ Mt. Everest •
❿ family •

• (a) 보통명사
• (b) 물질명사
• (c) 추상명사
• (d) 고유명사
• (e) 집합명사

Exercise

Exercise 1

보기에서 문맥과 어법에 맞는 단어를 골라 빈칸에 알맞은 형태로 바꿔 쓰세요.

보기 ① revolve ② candle ③ be ④ care ⑤ cheese

① How many ______ are on the birthday cake?

② Please help yourself to some ______.

③ The earth ______ around the sun.

④ Half a dozen people ______ riding bicycles.

⑤ The healthy ______ about the diet every single day.

Exercise 2

둘 중 맞는 단어를 골라 문장을 완성하세요.

① My brother fixed two **computer / computers** by himself.

② The Harry Potter movie is mostly about teen **fantasy / fantasies**.

③ The class **has / have** the latest air conditioner in the school.

④ All members of the dance club **was / were** fascinated by the performance.

⑤ **An employed / The employed** are taking skill-improving programs.

Exercise 3

빈칸을 채워 문장을 완성하세요.

❶ 경찰들은 미제사건의 범인을 쫓고 있다.
The police ______ chasing the criminal in the cold case. (be)

❷ Mary는 기말시험을 한 번에 통과하기 위해서 열성을 다하기 시작한다.
Mary ______ into overdrive to pass the final exam at once. (go)

❸ 스포츠 날을 위한 메달들은 금과 은으로 만들어진다.
The medals for the sports day event are made of ______ and silver.

❹ 나는 신학기를 준비하기 위해서 많은 책들과 옷들을 샀다.
I bought ______ books and clothes to get ready for the new semester.

❺ 많은 사람들이 공원에서 조깅과 요가를 하고 있다.
There ______ many people jogging and doing yoga at the park.

❻ 부상자들은 인근 병원에서 치료를 받았다.
The ______ were treated at a nearby hospital. (injure)

Sentence Completion

❶ A : I made paper ______. Do you want one?

B : They're so cute! I'd love one.

(A) doll
(B) dolls
(C) a dolls
(D) these doll

❷ A : Did you enjoy the book fair yesterday?

B : No. There ______ too many people at the fair.

(A) is
(B) are
(C) was
(D) were

❸ A : How much ______ those earrings?

B : Three dollars and fifty cents.

(A) is
(B) are
(C) was
(D) cost

❹ A : The ______ are feeding on the spacious grass and getting the warm sun.

B : How peaceful it is!

(A) car
(B) fox
(C) cow
(D) cattle

❺ A : I've recently been attracted to one drama. The main character is very mysterious.

B : ______ stimulate people's curiosity.

(A) Mystical
(B) A mystery
(C) A mystical
(D) The mystical

6 The social studies teacher has ______ information about this field in this school.

(A) few
(B) little
(C) much
(D) many

7 The crescent moon ______ so beautiful when the sky is pitch-black.

(A) is
(B) be
(C) are
(D) have

8 The committee ______ the final decision.

(A) is made
(B) are made
(C) has made
(D) have made

9 ______ are apt to get out of the trap easily regardless of how difficult it is.

(A) Clever
(B) A clever
(C) Be clever
(D) The clever

10 We should burn the midnight oil in order to attain ______ .

(A) impossible
(B) an impossible
(C) for impossible
(D) the impossible

Error Recognition

● TOSEL 기출문제 변형 수능/내신 출제유형

틀린 문장 고르기

다음 중 문법적으로 틀린 것을 고르세요.

The Galápagos iguana ① **is** the only sea lizard in the world. It lives on land but eats seaweed in the sea. The seaweed is found above the ② **water** but sometimes, the iguana dives into the sea to get the seaweed. When iguanas ③ **have** no food, they get shorter and thinner. They will get longer and fatter when they eat more food. There are about 200,000 – 300,000 iguanas in the Galápagos Islands. Many people in the Galapagos Islands ④ **coexists** with them and the good ⑤ **are** trying to protect them.

고쳐쓰기

틀린 문장을 쓰고 올바르게 고치세요.

→ ____________________

● TOSEL 기출문제 변형 수능/내신 출제유형

틀린 문장 고르기

다음 중 문법적으로 틀린 것을 고르세요.

① **Ratatouille** is a movie about a rat named Remy. He likes food a lot. He wants to become a chef. Everyone thinks that he is wanting ② **the impossible**. Remy ③ **find** himself in Gusteau's restaurant, an old, famous Parisian restaurant. Remy wants to cook and become a famous chef in ④ **Paris**. Remy must work with a clumsy boy named Lingini who works at Gusteau's. The food they make together ⑤ **is** so delicious that everyone wants it.

고쳐쓰기

틀린 문장을 쓰고 올바르게 고치세요.

→ ______________________

Unit Review

배운 내용 스스로 정리해보기

❶ 가산명사와 불가산명사

셀 수 있는 명사를 ❶ ______ (이)라고 하며 셀 수 없는 명사를 ❷ ______ (이)라고 한다.

예시문장 써보기

❶ ______ → ______

❷ ______ → ______

❷ 집합명사와 군집명사

구성원들이 모여 이루어진 집합체에 중점을 둔 것을 ❶ ______ (이)라고 하며,

집합체를 이루는 구성원에 중점을 둔 것을 ❷ ______ (이)라고 한다.

예시문장 써보기

❶ ______ → ______

❷ ______ → ______

❸ the + 형용사

예시문장 써보기

❶ 복수보통명사 → ______

❷ 단수보통명사 → ______

❸ 추상명사 → ______

UNIT 02

대명사

개념	사람이나 사물의 이름을 대신하여 가리키는 말 I drink water every day.
종류	❶ **인칭대명사** 주로 사람을 대신하여 가리키는 대명사로 인칭 수 격에 따라 종류가 달라짐 (it은 사물이나 내용을 대신하여 가리킴) Wendy and **I** like **him**. ❷ **부정대명사** 정해지지 않은 대상을 가리키는 대명사 **One** should have respect for the aged.

UNIT 2 대명사

1 인칭대명사

주격	소유격	목적격	소유대명사	재귀대명사
I	my	me	mine	myself
you	your	you	yours	yourself
he	his	him	his	himself
she	her	her	hers	herself
it	its	it	-	itself
we	our	us	ours	ourselves
you	your	you	yours	yourselves
they	their	them	theirs	themselves

- **My**(소유격) aunt gave **me**(목적격) **her**(소유격) old wallet.
- **Her**(소유격) voice is so nice that everyone loves **it**(목적격).
- **We**(주격) often forget the importance of **our**(소유격) family.
- **They**(주격) tried hard to fix the door **themselves**(재귀대명사).
- **I**(주격) know **myself**(재귀대명사) well than **you**(주격) do.

2 부정대명사

	대명사 단수	대명사 복수
불특정	another	others
특정	the other	the others
one·some	one	some

- I have two cars. One is blue and the other is red.
- He has five sons. One is in London and the others are in Japan.
- Some were dressed in blue, others black, others white, and etc.
- I have ten friends. Some are tall and the others are small.
- I don't like this hat. Show me another.

NOTE

TIP 부정대명사 심화

단어	뜻
both (of)	둘 다
neither (of)	둘 다 아니다
either (of)	둘 중 하나/둘 다

- Both of us were very tired.
- Neither answer is correct.
- You may eat either of them.

Activity

각 단어를 알맞은 인칭대명사와 연결시키세요.

① mine	
② them	
③ it	(a) 주격
④ yours	(b) 소유격
⑤ ourselves	(c) 목적격
⑥ your	
⑦ himself	(d) 소유대명사
⑧ ours	(e) 재귀대명사
⑨ him	
⑩ they	

Exercise

Exercise 1

그림을 보고 빈칸에 알맞은 표현을 보기에서 고르세요.

보기
- other flowers are yellow
- painting the wall by himself
- has to read them
- her granddaughter a present

❶ The grandmother gives ______________.

❷ There are lots of books. She ______________ until this week.

❸ Michael's uncle is ______________.

❹ Some flowers are red and ______________.

Exercise 2

둘 중 맞는 단어를 골라 문장을 완성하세요.

❶ I will introduce **myself / yourself** in front of my new classmates.

❷ He suggested issuing the membership cards, but I declined **it / them** .

❸ Could you pass me **theirs / his** scissors to cut the paper in halves?

❹ **We / Our** are trying to help children by teaching English at the kindergarten.

❺ There are two wallets. One is my father's and **another / the other** is mine.

Exercise 3

빈칸을 채워 문장을 완성하세요.

1. 내 친구들은 내 생일을 위해 깜짝 파티를 준비하고 있다.
   My friends are preparing for a surprise party for ______ birthday.

2. 학생들은 그들의 쉬는 시간에 그들 스스로 공부를 한다.
   The students are studying by ______ in their spare time.

3. 나는 지난주에 친구에게 시계를 빌려주었지만, 그가 나의 것을 어제 잃어버렸다.
   I lent my watch to my friend last week, but he lost ______ yesterday.

4. 장시간 컴퓨터 게임 하는 것은 우리를 컴퓨터 중독으로 이끈다.
   Playing computer games for a long time leads ______ to computer addiction.

5. 나는 오늘 “Shrek” 영화를 보고 싶지 않은데, 또 다른 영화는 없니?
   I don’t want to watch the “Shrek” movie today, is there ______ movie?

6. 너희 두 사람이 창문을 깼다고 들었어. 둘 다 따라와.
   I heard you two broke the window. Follow, ______ of you.

Sentence Completion

❶ A: Can you help ______ with this project?
B: Sure. Just tell me what you need me to do.

(A) I
(B) our
(C) me
(D) myself

❷ A: Whose dog is this? It's so cute.
B: It's my sister's. I'm taking care of ______ dog for two days.

(A) her
(B) his
(C) your
(D) their

❸ A : How old are your twin daughters?
B : ______ are six years old.

(A) She
(B) You
(C) They
(D) Ourselves

❹ A : Wow, this cake is so delicious! Did you bake it?
B : No, my grandmother baked it ______.

(A) she
(B) her
(C) hers
(D) herself

❺ A : I messed up my English exam. I am worthless.
B : It's okay. Don't beat ______ up too much.

(A) myself
(B) himself
(C) yourself
(D) ourselves

❻ ______ people may think whales are fish, but, in fact, they aren't.

(A) One
(B) Some
(C) Other
(D) The other

❼ Today I bought three sweaters. One is blue, ______ is yellow, and the other is pink.

(A) two
(B) other
(C) another
(D) the another

❽ I lost my cell phone yesterday. I think I have to buy a new ______.

(A) one
(B) other
(C) another
(D) the other

❾ Some think death penalty should be eliminated, but ______ think it shouldn't.

(A) one
(B) other
(C) others
(D) the other

❿ There are two copies of this document. One is in the library and ______ is in the museum.

(A) some
(B) other
(C) another
(D) the other

Error Recognition

● TOSEL 기출문제 변형 수능/내신 출제유형

틀린 문장 고르기

다음 중 문법적으로 틀린 것을 고르세요.

Tomorrow is the first day of school. I have to go to the store and buy ❶ **my** books and supplies. My new fourth-grade teacher has just sent ❷ **mine** the list of things that I will need. Most of the things are the same ❸ **ones** that I needed last year. But this year ❹ **I** need a special math set with a compass, protractor, and ruler. I really like math so I am excited to use the new ❺ **supplies** .

고쳐쓰기

틀린 문장을 쓰고 올바르게 고치세요.

→ ______________________

● TOSEL 기출문제 변형 수능/내신 출제유형

틀린 문장 고르기

다음 중 문법적으로 틀린 것을 고르세요.

This Christmas has been great. The whole family came home. ❶ **We** were all so excited to see each other. We didn't sleep but stayed up all night talking. The next day was Christmas Day and we got to open ❷ **us** presents. That's the best part of Christmas morning. I got lots of great presents from everyone. Grandma gave ❸ **me** a gold necklace. ❹ **My** mom and dad took lots of pictures. We ate a huge dinner that my father cooked ❺ **himself** . When it was finally time for bed I knew I'd had one of the best Christmases ever.

고쳐쓰기

틀린 문장을 쓰고 올바르게 고치세요.

→ ____________________

Unit Review

배운 내용 스스로 정리해보기

❶ 인칭대명사

수	인칭	주격	소유격	목적격	소유대명사	재귀대명사
단수	1인칭	I	my	me	mine	myself
	2인칭	you	your	you	yours	yourself
	3인칭	he	❶ ____	him	his	himself
		she	her	❷ ____	hers	herself
		it	its	it	-	itself
복수	1인칭	we	our	❸ ____	ours	ourselves
	2인칭	you	your	you	yours	❹ ____
	3인칭	they	❺ ____	them	theirs	themselves

예시문장 써보기

❶ his → ____________________

❷ her → ____________________

❸ ____ → ____________________

❷ 부정대명사

정해지지 않은 대상을 가리키는 대명사를 ____ 라고 한다.

빈칸에 알맞은 부정대명사 쓰기

❶ ____ of the twins is a girl. ____ is a boy.

❷ ____ wore blue hats, ____ wore red hats, white hats, and etc.

UNIT 03

형용사

개념

사람이나 사물의 모양이나 성질을 나타내는 말

This is an **important** decision.

종류

❶ **한정적 용법:** 명사의 앞이나 뒤에서 명사를 직접 수식하는 경우

It's a **golden** ring. (O)

The ring is **golden**. (X)

❷ **전치수식과 후치수식**

He gave an **interesting** talk.

Tell me something **interesting** about yourself.

❸ **수량형용사:** 수나 양을 나타내는 형용사

	조금 있는	거의 없는	많은	
가산명사	a few	few	many	a lot of, lots of
불가산명사	a little	little	much	

UNIT 3 형용사

1 한정적 용법

It was just a **mere** accident.

This is a **wooden** table which my grandfather made for me.

2 전치수식과 후치수식

❶ 전치수식

He cannot finish it in such a **short** time.

I know a **handsome** guy.

We had such a **good** time at the seaside.

❷ 후치수식

There lived a king **anxious** for his people's welfare.

I met **a man** seventy-five years old.
= I met a seventy-five-year-old man.

I have answered at the letter **received**.

3 수량형용사

❶ many vs. much

Many children have made the same mistakes.
복수 보통명사

I really don't have **much** money.
단수 물질명사

❷ (a) few vs. (a) little

He has **few** friends.

You still have **a little** time left.

NOTE

TIP 한정적 용법

- 명사의 앞이나 뒤에서 명사를 직접 수식하는 경우를 말한다.

TIP 서술적 용법

- 형용사가 보어로 쓰일 경우를 말한다.
Her idea was great.

TIP 용어 설명

- 전치수식 : 형용사 → 명사
- 후치수식 : 명사 ← 형용사

TIP

- a lot of, lots of, some은 가산명사, 불가산명사 모두에 쓰일 수 있다.

Activity

각 문장의 형용사에 대해 가장 알맞은 유형을 고르세요.

❶ My family gave me a <u>lovely</u> piano as a present.
(전치수식, 후치수식)

❷ This curriculum is the one <u>different</u> from the former.
(전치수식, 후치수식)

❸ The zookeeper takes care of sick animals <u>screaming</u>.
(전치수식, 후치수식)

❹ There is lots of <u>delicious</u> food on the table.
(전치수식, 후치수식)

❺ I think this problem was not a big deal. It was just a <u>mere</u> mistake.
(한정적 용법, 서술적 용법)

❻ Margot wore a <u>beautiful</u> hat to the pie-eating contest.
(한정적 용법, 서술적 용법)

❼ I don't think she seems <u>nice</u> at all.
(한정적 용법, 서술적 용법)

Exercise

Exercise 1

아래 보기에서 문맥에 맞는 형용사를 골라 (A), (B) 중 적절한 위치의 빈칸에 써넣으세요.

보기 ❶ dangerous ❷ many ❸ little ❹ mad

❶ Playing ball on the road is a (A) ______ behavior (B) ______.

❷ There was (A) ______ food (B) ______ in the fridge.

❸ The young girl has (A) ______ books (B) ______ about birds.

❹ Your excuse will only make (A) ______ her (B) ______.

Exercise 2

둘 중 맞는 단어를 골라 문장을 완성하세요.

❶ The old man in the subway looks like a **lonely / loneliness** person.

❷ I try to get hold of someone **be / being** able to listen to my opinion.

❸ Promoting cosmetics on social media is **many / much** pleasure for me.

❹ The regular customers got **many / much** giveaways at the department store.

❺ We had an **enjoy / enjoyable** time with Bob and Helen.

Exercise 3

괄호 안의 단어를 적절하게 변형하여 빈칸을 채워 문장을 완성하세요.

❶ 나는 어려운 문제를 다루고 싶다.
I would like to deal with the ________ problem. (challenge)

❷ Louis 박사는 낯선 누군가를 데리고 회의에 들어갔다.
Dr. Louis entered the conference with someone ________ . (strange)

❸ 그녀는 옷에 관해서라면 화려한 어떤 것이든 좋아하는 경향이 있다.
She tends to like ________ fancy when it comes to clothes. (any)

❹ 많은 사람들이 저작물들을 무분별하게 배포함으로써 저작권을 경시한다.
________ people disregard copyright by distributing literary productions thoughtlessly. (lot)

❺ 사람들은 그 게임을 매우 재미있고 흥미롭다고 여긴다.
People find the game very fun and ________ . (interest)

❻ 그 권투선수는 상대에게 강력한 펀치를 날려서 그를 기절시켰다.
The boxer hit a ________ punch to his opponent and knocked him out. (power)

Sentence Completion

❶ A : I heard that you went out with Sean the other night. How was it?

B : We had ________ a good time.

(A) so
(B) that
(C) such
(D) what

❷ A : Have you seen ________ of oranges around here?

B : No, I haven't. Why do you ask?

(A) a box full
(B) full a box
(C) a full box
(D) box full a

❸ A : What did you buy at the flea market?

B : I bought these ________ dolls made in Japan.

(A) wood
(B) woods
(C) woody
(D) wooden

❹ A : Wow, That was an ________ show!

B : Yes, it really was. I want to see it again.

(A) excel
(B) excellent
(C) excellently
(D) excellented

❺ A: Do you have any pencils?

B: Yes, I have ________ of them.

(A) such
(B) a few
(C) a little
(D) neither

6 I have never tasted ______ a delicious cake in my whole life!

(A) so
(B) very
(C) such
(D) what

7 There once lived a boy ______ about making mistakes.

(A) anxiety
(B) clumsy
(C) anxious
(D) clumsily

8 We stayed in a ______ castle in France.

(A) beauty
(B) beauties
(C) beautiful
(D) beautifully

9 Sometimes we just need ______ time for ourselves.

(A) few
(B) little
(C) a few
(D) a little

10 We don't need ______ money in order to be happy.

(A) few
(B) little
(C) many
(D) much

Error Recognition

● TOSEL 기출문제 변형 수능/내신 출제유형

틀린 문장 고르기

다음 중 문법적으로 틀린 것을 고르세요.

Welcome to the channel five weather report. You have a ① **great** week ahead. It will be hot and sunny all week. Monday is a day to see the ② **perfectly** sky. Wednesday ③ **is** a great day to go to the beach. But on the weekend there will be ④ **lots of** rain. Saturday would be a great day to see that ⑤ **new** movie about penguins. Have a great week!

고쳐쓰기

틀린 문장을 쓰고 올바르게 고치세요.

→ ________________

● TOSEL 기출문제 변형 수능/내신 출제유형

틀린 문장 고르기

다음 중 문법적으로 틀린 것을 고르세요.

Contact lenses are ① **tiny** lenses that are worn on ② **your** eye. Like glasses, they improve the wearer's vision. This type of lens was thought of by Leonardo da Vinci in 1508 and later by René Descartes around 1636-1637. Contact lenses were finally invented and made in 1887 by a German, Adolf Eugen Fick. ③ **He** first made lenses for animals, and later for people. The lenses were made from heavy ④ **brown** glass and were 18-21mm in diameter. The lenses were improved by August Muller in 1889; he made lenses that were ⑤ **smallest** than in the past.

고쳐쓰기

틀린 문장을 쓰고 올바르게 고치세요.

→ ______________________

Unit Review

배운 내용 스스로 정리해보기

❶ 한정적 용법

꾸며주는 대상을 앞이나 뒤에서 수식하여 그 의미를 한정해주는 용법을 ______(이)라고 한다.

예시문장 써보기

______ ➔ ______

❷ 전치수식과 후치수식

대상을 앞에서 꾸며주는 것을 ❶ ______, 뒤에서 꾸며주는 것을 ❷ ______(이)라고 한다.

예시문장 써보기

❶ ______ ➔ ______

❷ ______ ➔ ______

❸ 수량형용사

수량형용사는 수나 양을 나타내는 형용사로 꾸밈을 받는 명사가 ❶ ______ 여부와 ❷ ______ 에 따라 쓰임이 달라진다.

예시문장 써보기

❶ few ➔ ______

❷ a few ➔ ______

❸ little ➔ ______

❹ a little ➔ ______

UNIT 04

감탄사

개념	놀람, 느낌, 부름, 응답 등을 나타내는 말 Oh my god!
감탄문	How 또는 What으로 시작하여 느낌표로 마치는 문장으로, How와 What은 very의 뜻을 나타냄 ❶ How How kind she is! ❷ What What a kind girl she is!

1 감탄사

Wow, that sounds great! Let's try it.

Oops, I accidentally stepped on your bag.

Well, I guess you can say so.

Ouch, that hurt! Stop doing that.

Uh oh, he is heading the wrong way.

Aww, your cat is so adorable!

Eww! Swallow your food before talking!

Gosh, that was mean.

NOTE

2 감탄문

❶ How + 형용사 [부사] + 주어 + 동사 !

How beautiful this flower is!
(How: 의문사 / beautiful: 형용사 / this flower: 주어 / is: 동사)

❷ What + a(an) + 형용사 + 명사 + 주어 + 동사 !

What a clever puppy he is!
(What: 의문사 / a: 부정관사 / clever: 형용사 / puppy: 명사 / he: 주어 / is: 동사)

Activity

주어진 문장을 감탄문과 감탄문이 아닌 것으로 구분해보세요. (O , X)

1. Oh my god! ( )
2. He was very surprised by the fact. ( )
3. Uh oh, he is heading to the wrong way. ( )
4. How beautiful she is! ( )
5. She is always kind to everyone. ( )
6. Gosh, that was mean. ( )
7. Well, I guess you can say so. ( )
8. It is a very fun book. ( )
9. What a smart girl! ( )
10. What is she eating? ( )

Exercise

Exercise 1

빈칸의 단어를 바르게 배열하여 알맞은 감탄문을 만들어보세요.

❶ 그것은 정말 좋은 아이디어야! (idea / brilliant / a / what / is / it)
→

❷ 그녀는 정말 운이 좋구나! (lucky / How / she / is)
→

❸ 그가 얼마나 친절한 소년인지! (boy / kind / a / what / is / he)
→

❹ 오, 그거 정말 좋다! (Wow / great / sounds / that)
→

❺ 그는 정말 영리한 강아지이다! (dog / clever / what / he / is / a)
→

Exercise 2

둘 중 맞는 감탄사를 고르세요.

❶ **What / How** a clever girl she is!

❷ **Wow / Ouch** , that hurts! Stop doing that.

❸ **What / How** a surprising ending it is!

❹ **Well / Oops** , I accidentally stepped on your bag

❺ **What / How** fun books they are!

Exercise 3

다음 문장을 감탄문으로 바꿔 쓰세요.

❶ This flower is very beautiful. (how)

➡

❷ She is a very smart girl. (what)

➡

❸ It is a very interesting question. (what)

➡

❹ He was very sad. (how)

➡

❺ It is a very amazing place. (what)

➡

Sentence Completion

❶ A : ______, it hurts!

B : Oh my god! Are you okay?

(A) Wow
(B) Ouch
(C) Oops
(D) Gosh

❷ A : How's your project going?

B : ______, I'm thinking of new solutions.

(A) Aww
(B) Eww
(C) Well
(D) Ouch

❸ A : Look at those beautiful roses! ______ beautiful they are!

B : Wow, they really are.

(A) How
(B) What
(C) When
(D) How much

❹ A : Did you draw this? What ______ painting it is!

B : Thank you. You flatter me.

(A) beautiful a
(B) a beautiful
(C) beautifully a
(D) a beautifully

❺ A: I made these cookies. Would you like to try some?

B: Wow, ______ delicious!

(A) how
(B) how a
(C) what
(D) what a

6 ________, the stars above the sky are twinkling!

(A) Wow
(B) Well
(C) Ouch
(D) Uh oh

7 ________, I think I dropped my wallet somewhere on the street.

(A) Eww
(B) Wow
(C) Oops
(D) Ouch

8 Did you see Anna's smile? ________ she is!

(A) How love
(B) What love
(C) How lovely
(D) What lovely

9 It is sunny and breezy today. ________ nice day to go on a picnic!

(A) How a
(B) What
(C) A what
(D) What a

10 You just need to press this button to unlock. ________ it is!

(A) How simple
(B) Very simple
(C) So a simple
(D) What a simple

Error Recognition

● TOSEL 기출문제 변형 수능/내신 출제유형

틀린 문장 고르기

다음 중 문법적으로 틀린 것을 고르세요.

Space Camp ❶ **uses** space to excite and teach children ages 9-11 about math, science, and technology. Teamwork and communication will be learned from ❷ **many** missions like rocket building, and robotics. The cost of a week camp is $700. ❸ **It** includes meals, room, and activities. Everything you need will be ❹ **perfectly** prepared. Try space food, learn to sleep in space, and even how to go to the bathroom in space. ❺ **How** a special experience this would be!

고쳐쓰기

틀린 문장을 쓰고 올바르게 고치세요.

→ ______________________

● TOSEL 기출문제 변형 수능/내신 출제유형

틀린 문장 고르기

다음 중 문법적으로 틀린 것을 고르세요.

Pick your pen pal. Mary, 24 years old, ① **comes** from Scotland and would like to have a pen pal who is from Europe. ② **She** likes playing the piano and listening to jazz music. She is interested in history and ③ **old** movies. Pietro, 42 years old, comes from Argentina. He is a businessman and would like to find a pen pal who is also a businessperson and lives in North America. He is married, has three children and likes using the Internet in his ④ **free** time. What a ⑤ **variously** people there are!

고쳐쓰기

틀린 문장을 쓰고 올바르게 고치세요.

→ ______________________

Unit Review

배운 내용 스스로 정리해보기

❶ 감탄사

놀람, 느낌, 부름, 응답 등을 나타내는 말을 ________ (이)라고 한다.

예시문장 써보기

________ → ________________________________

❷ 감탄문

감탄문은 놀람, 기쁨, 슬픔 등의 감정과 느낌 등을 나타내며
❶ ________ 또는 ❷ ________ (으)로 시작하여 ❸ ________ (으)로 마치는 문장이다.

평서문을 감탄문으로 고쳐보기

"He is very generous man."

❶ How → ________________________________

❷ What → ________________________________

TOSEL 실전문제 1

PART 6. Sentence Completion

DIRECTIONS: In this portion of the test, you will be given 10 incomplete sentences. From the choices provided, choose the word or words that correctly complete the sentence. Then, fill in the corresponding space on your answer sheet.

1. A: These ______ are so fancy!
   B: I agree! I made them.

   (A) ribbon
   (B) ribbons
   (C) a ribbon
   (D) the ribbon

2. A: What happened with the museum trip yesterday?
   B: ______ signed up, so it was cancelled.

   (A) No one
   (B) Another
   (C) The others
   (D) Everywhere

3. A: This song is so good!
   B: It's one of ______ favorites.

   (A) we
   (B) my
   (C) ours
   (D) mine

4. A: Why don't we go to the fine restaurant today?
   B: Sorry, I can't afford it. I don't have ______ money.

   (A) no
   (B) few
   (C) many
   (D) much

5. A: It only takes five seconds to complete downloading the program.
   B: ______ it is!

   (A) Fast
   (B) How fast
   (C) Very fast
   (D) What a fast

6. It is widely believed that ______ are brave, but I don't agree with that.

(A) young
(B) a young
(C) the young
(D) they young

7. We should keep in mind the importance of _____ new project.

(A) our
(B) their
(C) your
(D) other

8. Oh my god, it's so hot outside. Please give us something ______ to drink.

(A) cold
(B) a cold
(C) cold water
(D) the thing cold

9. I just finished watching the new 'Avengers' movie. _____ movie it is!

(A) Awesome
(B) How awesome
(C) What awesome
(D) What an awesome

10. ______, I think I forgot to turn the lights off my room. I need to go back.

(A) Wow
(B) Eww
(C) Oops
(D) Ouch

Error Recognition

1. 다음 중 문법적으로 틀린 것을 골라 고치세요.

• TOSEL 기출문제 변형 수능/내신 출제유형

1

Sofie's family loves Christmas. ① **They** have many special traditions in their family. Some of ② **their** traditions are the same as other families and some are completely different. Every Christmas, they visit her grandmother. They sit around a fire and drink egg nog and tell funny stories about the last year. ③ **She** grandmother always has the funniest stories. On Christmas eve, everyone in the family opens one gift.

→ ______________________

2. 다음 밑줄 친 부분을 바르게 고치세요.

● TOSEL 기출문제 변형 수능/내신 출제유형

2

Tigers coats are usually orange with darker stripes. The stripes can vary in color from dark brown to black. A tiger's stripes are much like fingerprints in humans. **Two tigers no** have the same set of stripes. In fact, when someone shaves a tiger, his fur grows back with the same stripes it had before.

→ ______________________

CHAPTER 02

II. 8품사 (2)

UNIT 01

동사

개념	주어의 동작이나 상태를 나타내는 말 He **runs** fast.
시제	❶ 기본시제: 현재, 과거, 미래 I **will** **walk**. ❷ 진행시제: 현재진행, 과거진행, 미래진행 I **am** **walking**.
조동사	동사를 도와서 필요, 의무, 가능 등을 나타냄 You **can** **reserve** seats.

1 자동사와 타동사

자동사	완전자동사 Her opinion matters. (주어: Her opinion / 동사: matters) 불완전자동사 This chocolate cake smells good. (주어: This chocolate cake / 동사: smells / 보어(형용사): good)
타동사	She eats hamburger and pizza for dinner. (주어: She / 동사: eats / 목적어: hamburger and pizza)

2 혼동하기 쉬운 자동사와 타동사

❶ 타동사로 혼동하기 쉬운 자동사

He graduated from high school.

≠ He graduated high school. (X)

❷ 자동사로 혼동하기 쉬운 타동사

Alice married my cousin brother.

≠ Alice married with my cousin brother. (X)

3 동사의 수일치

상관 접속사	뜻	동사의 수일치
not A but B	A가 아니라 B	B에 일치
not only A but also B (=B as well as A)	A뿐만 아니라 B도	B에 일치
either A or B	A 혹은 B	B에 일치
neither A nor B	A와 B 둘 다 아닌	B에 일치
both A and B	A와 B 둘 다	복수 동사

Not you but she is wrong.

Not only she but also I am interested in politics.

Either I or she is going to be at home tomorrow.

NOTE

TIP 수여동사로 혼동하기 쉬운 3형식동사

- Mr. Wang explained the decision to me.

≠ Mr. Wang explained me the decision. (X)

TIP 자동사 + 전치사

단어	뜻
Agree to	~에 동의하다
Apologize to	~에 사과하다
Arrive at	~에 도착하다
Complain of	~을 불평하다
Consent to	~를 동의하다
Interfere with	~를 방해하다
Reply to	~에 답하다
Listen to	~를 듣다
Look for	~를 찾다
Wait for	~를 기다리다

TIP 타동사

단어	뜻
Attend	~에 참석하다
Discuss	~에 대해 토론하다
Enter	~에 들어가다
Leave	~을 떠나다
Mention	~에 대해 언급하다
Reach	~에 도달하다
Resemble	~와 닮다

TIP all

- 명사에 따라 단수/복수 동사

TIP every

- 항상 단수

Activity

각 단어를 알맞은 동사와 연결시키세요.

❶ matter •	
❷ smell •	
❸ eat •	• (a) 자동사
❹ walk •	
❺ marry •	
❻ graduate •	
❼ discuss •	
❽ explain •	• (b) 타동사
❾ hold •	
❿ enter •	

Exercise

Exercise 1

보기에서 알맞은 것을 고라 문장을 완성하세요.

보기 ① ø (전치사 없음) ② for ③ on ④ from ⑤ with ⑥ to

① I can't wait ______ my birthday.

② We are planning to attend ______ the meeting about the project.

③ You should apologize ______ her about your misbehavior.

④ Before entering ______ the building, make sure to sanitize your hand.

⑤ I want you to stop interfering ______ me and leave me alone.

Exercise 2

둘 중 어법에 맞는 것을 고르세요.

① She closely resembles **ø / to** her mother.

② Rachel congratulated her son **ø / on** graduating top of his class.

③ He is looking **for / ø** a missing pen.

④ My younger brother asked **ø / to** me a math question.

⑤ She reminded **ø / to** me of my schedule next week.

Exercise 3

빈칸을 채워 문장을 완성하세요.

❶ 내 남자 형제와 여자 형제는 모두 은행에서 일한다. (work)
Both my sister and my brother ______ at a bank.

❷ 그녀뿐 아니라 나 역시 과학에 흥미가 있다. (be)
Not only she but also I ______ interested in science.

❸ Tim과 Grace 모두 요리하는 것을 좋아한다. (enjoy)
Both Tim and Grace ______ cooking.

❹ 나뿐만 아니라 그 역시 영어를 매일 공부하고 있다. (be)
He as well as I ______ studying English every day.

❺ 나 또는 그녀가 내일 집에 있을 것이다. (be)
Either I or she ______ going to be at home tomorrow.

❻ 병원에 있는 모든 환자들이 그 질병으로 고통받는다. (suffer)
All patients in the hospital ______ from the disease.

Sentence Completion

❶ A : What did Mr. Park say to you? He seemed serious.

B : Nothing much. He explained ______ .

(A) me the situation

(B) the situation to me

(C) to me the situation

(D) me to the situation

❷ A : My grandmother made some japchae for me.

B : Wow, it ______ delicious.

(A) sees

(B) eats

(C) looks

(D) likes

❸ A : When did you ______ the college?

B : About five years ago.

(A) graduate

(B) graduation

(C) graduate for

(D) graduate from

❹ A : Wow, I can't believe Mary is going to ______ Steve tomorrow.

B : I know. Time flies.

(A) marry

(B) marry to

(C) marry with

(D) married to

❺ A: Who likes Jane, Tim or James?

B : Neither Tim nor James ______ Jane.

(A) like

(B) likes

(C) is liked

(D) are liked

❻ Henry's grandmother passed away yesterday. He ________ depressed.

(A) eats
(B) looks
(C) matters
(D) seems like

❼ I don't understand why Jake is unemployed. He ________ hard.

(A) works
(B) keeps
(C) drinks
(D) drives

❽ Call me when you ________ the airport. I will pick you up.

(A) arrive
(B) arrive at
(C) arrive to
(D) arrive with

❾ Chris ________ his father very much. Sometimes his mother can't tell the difference.

(A) resembles
(B) resembles to
(C) resembles with
(D) resembles between

❿ Both Sharon and Joon ________ Spanish fluently. They lived in Madrid when they were little.

(A) speak
(B) speaks
(C) spoken
(D) are spoken

Error Recognition

● TOSEL 기출문제 변형 수능/내신 출제유형

틀린 문장 고르기

다음 중 문법적으로 틀린 것을 고르세요.

Martin Luther King Jr. worked to make a ① **better** world for African-Americans. He was born on January 15, 1929, in Atlanta, Georgia. Martin was an ② **excellent** student in school. Martin ③ **entered** Morehouse College at the age of 15. He decided to do something to make the world a better and fairer place. After ④ **graduating** college and getting married, Dr. King became a minister and moved to Alabama. Dr. King was killed on April 4, 1968. Each year in January, the month in which he was born, there is a day to ⑤ **commemorate** him.

고쳐쓰기

틀린 문장을 쓰고 올바르게 고치세요.

→ ______________________

● TOSEL 기출문제 변형 수능/내신 출제유형

틀린 문장 고르기

다음 중 문법적으로 틀린 것을 고르세요.

This is a story about two ① **birds** . Vatiman and Vasil were good friends. Vatiman was green and white. Vasil was all black. One day Vatiman decided that he would like to be more colorful. He looked for something he could use to dye ② **his** feathers. He finally found a red leaf. He dug a hole and filled it with ③ **red** leaves. Vatiman was very happy. He ④ **left from** there to go get cleaned before jumping in the red dye. However, after he came back, most of the red-dyed water was gone! Then he saw Vasil. Not Vatiman but Vasil ⑤ **was** dyeing his hair colorful. Vatiman was sad and angry because now Vasil was more colorful than he was. Vatiman no longer wanted to be friends with Vasil.

고쳐쓰기

틀린 문장을 쓰고 올바르게 고치세요.

→ ________________

Unit Review

배운 내용 스스로 정리해보기

❶ 자동사와 타동사

목적어를 취하지 않는 동사를 ❶ ________, 취하는 동사를 ❷ ________(이)라고 한다.

예시문장 써보기

❶ ________ → ________________

❷ ________ → ________________

❷ 혼동하기 쉬운 자동사와 타동사

예시문장 써보기

❶ 타동사로 혼동하기 쉬운 자동사 → ________________

❷ 자동사로 혼동하기 쉬운 타동사 → ________________

❸ 동사의 수일치

예시문장 써보기

❶ not only A but (also) B → ________________

❷ Neither A nor B → ________________

UNIT 02

부사

개념	**다른 말을 도와 장소, 시간, 방법, 이유 등을 나타내는 말로, 주로 형용사, 동사, 부사, 문장 전체를 꾸며줌** I wrote the report **quickly**.
생김새	**① 형용사 + ly** The man **slowly** drank a bottle of water. **② 형용사와 동일** She works **hard**.

1 부사의 형태

She could find the answer **easily**.
형용사 + ly

= The answer was **easy** to find (for her).
형용사

The number of tourists increased **dramatically**.
형용사 + ly

2 형용사와 형태가 같은 부사

I saw a **fast** rabbit while climbing.
형용사

The rabbit runs **fast**.
부사

3 ly가 붙어 전혀 뜻이 다른 부사로 되는 경우

❶ hard / hardly

He studied very **hard**. 열심히

He **hardly** studied. 거의 ~하지 않다

❷ right / rightly

You must go **right** now. 바로 (지금)

You must understand it **rightly**. 정확하게

❷ free / freely

You can eat for **free** in his restaurant. 무료로

He will give you anything **freely**. 아낌없이, 기꺼이

NOTE

TIP 형용사와 형태가 같은 부사

- early, long, far, half, straight, ill, well, much, little, very, low, etc.

Activity

단어가 형용사인지 부사인지 골라보세요.

1. rapid •
2. happily •
3. sharply •
4. nearly •
5. endless •
6. forgetful •
7. carefully •
8. friendly •
9. lovely •
10. bad •

• (a) 형용사

• (b) 부사

UNIT 2 부사

Exercise

Exercise 1

주어진 형용사를 부사 형태로 바꿔보세요.

1. The world changes **rapid**.
→

2. My children are playing **happy**.
→

3. She could find the answer **easy**.
→

4. She performed **beautiful** on the ice rink.
→

Exercise 2

둘 중 맞는 단어를 고르세요.

1. 그는 하루 종일 열심히 공부했다.
He studied **hard / hardly** all day long.

2. 나는 최근에 두통을 앓고 있다.
I have been having some headaches **late / lately** .

3. 이 책은 매우 높은 가격에 팔렸다.
This book was sold at a **high / highly** price.

4. 그가 너에게 무엇이든 아낌없이 줄 것이다.
He will give you anything **free / freely** .

Exercise 3

밑줄 친 단어의 품사를 구분해보세요.

❶ I really worked **hard** to get a good score on the exam.

➡

This chair is so **hard** that I couldn't use it anymore.

➡

❷ She runs very **fast**.

➡

I hope that he will make a **fast** recovery.

➡

❸ They had an **early** dinner.

➡

The sun sets **early** in winter.

➡

❹ She has **long** hair.

➡

I studied all night **long** to prepare for the quiz.

➡

❺ We went to bed **late** last night.

➡

I'm sorry I'm **late**.

➡

Sentence Completion

❶ A : I woke up at 6 today.

B : Why did you get up so ______?

(A) earl
(B) early
(C) earlily
(D) earlingly

❷ A : What do you think about Kristen?

B : I think she is ______ nice.

(A) real
(B) really
(C) realily
(D) a real

❸ A : Can you do a cartwheel?

B : I tried, but I couldn't. It's too ______ for me.

(A) hard
(B) hardly
(C) harder
(D) hardness

❹ A : Did you enjoy watching the F1 race?

B : Not really. Cars were running so ______, so the noise was very loud.

(A) fast
(B) slow
(C) fastly
(D) slowly

❺ A: Where have you been? I was looking for you all day long!

B : I was standing ______ here.

(A) right
(B) rights
(C) rightly
(D) righting

6 **Randy and his teammates won the game ________. Everybody cheered happily.**

(A) perfect
(B) perfectly
(C) perfecter
(D) perfection

7 **You just need to ________ copy sentences from the former document.**

(A) simply
(B) simple
(C) simpler
(D) simplicity

8 **I haven't seen her ________. Rumor has it that she has gone to Japan.**

(A) late
(B) later
(C) latter
(D) lately

9 **Orangutans in this shelter are allowed to move ________.**

(A) free
(B) freely
(C) not free
(D) not freely

10 **My phone seems to be broken. I can ________ hear voices while I am on the phone.**

(A) hard
(B) harder
(C) hardly
(D) hardlier

Error Recognition

● TOSEL 기출문제 변형 수능/내신 출제유형

틀린 문장 고르기

다음 중 문법적으로 틀린 것을 고르세요.

Dogs make great pets. One popular dog is the Chihuahua. They are a dog that many people ① **believe** is from Mexico, but its origin can be traced back to China. Chihuahuas are ② **quick** and clever dogs. They are also the smallest breed of dog. Chihuahuas enjoy love and attention. They are ③ **very** loyal to their owners. They are ④ **easy** trained. Chihuahuas weigh an average of three to five pounds. Their ⑤ **light** weight makes them a great travel partner.

고쳐쓰기

틀린 문장을 쓰고 올바르게 고치세요.

→ ____________________

● TOSEL 기출문제 변형 수능/내신 출제유형

틀린 문장 고르기

다음 중 문법적으로 틀린 것을 고르세요.

Sofie's family loves Christmas. They have many special traditions in their family. Some of their traditions are the same as other families and some are ① **completely** different. Every Christmas they visit her grandmother. They ② **sit** around a fire and drink eggnog and tell funny stories about the last year. Her grandmother always gives them the funniest stories ③ **free** . On Christmas eve everyone in the family is allowed to open one gift. The only rule is the person who gave the gift must be there. Sofie's Mom opens ④ **her** gift first, then her dad opens his gift. Sofie is the one who takes pictures. She thinks pictures are important because they're a great way to remember a ⑤ **wonderful** holiday.

고쳐쓰기

틀린 문장을 쓰고 올바르게 고치세요.

→ ______________________

Unit Review

배운 내용 스스로 정리해보기

❶ 부사의 형태

부사는 주로 형용사에 ______(을)를 붙인 형태이다.

예시문장 써보기

❶ 형용사에 ly를 붙인 부사 → ______

❷ 형용사 어미의 y를 i로 바꾸고 ly를 붙인 부사 → ______

❷ 형용사와 형태가 같은 부사

예시문장 써보기

→ ______

→ ______

❸ ly가 붙어 전혀 뜻이 다른 부사로 되는 경우

예시문장 써보기

❶ hard → ______

❷ hardly → ______

UNIT 03

전치사

개념	**명사나 대명사 앞에서 다른 요소와의 관계를 나타내는 말** The cat is **on the sofa.**
쓰임	① **시간: in, at, on 등** I was born **in 2008.** Let us meet **at 8 o'clock.** ② **방향·장소: up, in, at, on 등** He ran **up the stairs.** He is **in the living room.**

전치사의 종류

to	He is on the way **to** school. (전치사구(to + 명사)) I am starving **to** death. This is the key **to** that house.
on	You should write it **on** the paper. (전치사구(on + 명사)) **On** New Year's Day, I will visit my grandmother. The supermarket is **on** the right.
in	I will travel **in** Japan. (전치사구(in + 명사)) We will be back **in** an hour. He spilled a cup of juice **in** all directions.
at	Her puppy stands **at** the door. (전치사구(at + 명사)) You must never throw stones **at** animals. Let's study together tomorrow **at** noon.
of	He died **of** cancer. (전치사구(of + 명사)) You can choose one **of** the books she brought. It's good to keep the love **of** art.
with	I live **with** my grandparents. (전치사구(to + 명사)) What is the matter **with** you? Mrs. Kim is pleased **with** her son's letter.

NOTE

TIP 그 밖에 자주 쓰이는 전치사들

단어	뜻
through	~을 통해
for	위한, 위해
since	~부터 [이후]
behind	뒤에, 뒤떨어져
about	~에 대한/~에 관한

Activity

공통으로 쓰이는 전치사를 보기에서 골라 아래 빈칸에 적으세요.

보기 to on in at by with

❶	_______ 7 o'clock
	_______ midnight
	_______ 11:45 A.M.
❷	_______ Sunday/Monday
	_______ 17 July
	_______ New Year's Day
❸	_______ summer/spring
	_______ April/November
	_______ 1999/2017
❹	_______ the table
	_______ the grass
	_______ the ceiling
❺	way _______ school
	come _______ our house
❻	go _______ me
	a house _______ a big garden
❼	go _______ plane
	bitten _______ a dog
❽	I'm staying _______ home.
	I met her _______ a party.

Exercise

Exercise 1

다음 괄호에서 가장 알맞은 단어를 고르세요.

1. 이것이 저 방의 열쇠이므로, 이것을 잃어버리지 않도록 해라.
   This is the key **on / to** that room, so make sure not to lose it.
2. 현관에 누군가가 있다.
   Someone is **by / at** the front door.
3. 과학을 사랑하는 마음을 가지고 있는 것이 좋다.
   It's good to keep the love **with / of** science.
4. 나는 나의 조부모님과 함께 산다.
   I live **with / in** my grandparents.

Exercise 2

밑줄 친 부분을 올바른 전치사로 바꿔보세요.

1. I am very fond **with** drinking coffee.
   →
2. I was satisfied **to** the test result.
   →
3. My sister is married **by** a famous actor.
   →
4. Surprisingly, she specializes **on** mechanical engineering.
   →

Exercise 3

빈칸에 공통으로 들어갈 알맞은 전치사를 써넣으세요.

1. He sent our wedding photos to us ______ e-mail.
   I was amazed ______ the spectacular landscape.

2. I am so worried ______ the presentation tomorrow.
   Her son was curious ______ everything, so he kept asking questions to her.

3. He is responsible for taking care ______ his children.
   They were not aware ______ the rules, so they got punished.

4. This dress is similar ______ what you recommended last month.
   This theory applies ______ all of the phenomenons concerning the electron.

5. Switzerland is famous ______ its beautiful mountains.
   I have to pay ______ the room service that I ordered.

Sentence Completion

❶ A : How was your weekend?

B : I went to Seoul. I was amazed by the view ______ the 63 building.

(A) to
(B) at
(C) for
(D) with

❷ A : Could I talk with you ______ just a minute?

B : Sure. I am not in a hurry to leave.

(A) to
(B) on
(C) for
(D) with

❸ A : Where is your locker key?

B : It fell ______ a hole in my bag. It's gone.

(A) at
(B) up
(C) below
(D) through

❹ A : What time shall we meet tomorrow?

B : Well, let's meet ______ noon.

(A) at
(B) in
(C) on
(D) for

❺ A : What's the matter ______ Kate? She seems upset.

B : She lost her purse.

(A) of
(B) on
(C) with
(D) above

6. It was my first time I've been ______ Europe. I was so excited to visit all the museums.

(A) in
(B) on
(C) at
(D) for

7. ______ Christmas day, people leave cookies and milk for Santa Claus.

(A) In
(B) On
(C) At
(D) For

8. We are going to take a sightseeing bus ______ the morning, and then we are having lunch at a fancy restaurant.

(A) at
(B) on
(C) in
(D) for

9. Please show me one ______ your most valuable artworks.

(A) of
(B) at
(C) for
(D) with

10. I used to live ______ three roommates. It was horrible.

(A) in
(B) to
(C) for
(D) with

Error Recognition

● TOSEL 기출문제 변형 수능/내신 출제유형

틀린 문장 고르기

다음 중 문법적으로 틀린 것을 고르세요.

I love to travel. It's my favorite hobby. I've been to many different countries. Egypt is one ① **at** my favorite places to visit. I enjoy seeing the pyramids and the Sphynx. They are ② **in** the middle of a big desert. I like visiting France too. The Eiffel Tower is amazing. It's very tall, and it's in the middle of a ③ **great** city, Paris! I like Thailand too. Bangkok is a ④ **very** busy city. There are many people and lots of things to do. Thai food is very delicious, and it's cheap too. When I'm in Thailand I like to ⑤ **visit** all their beautiful beaches. The water is warm and clean. There are many more places I'd like to visit. I wonder where I can go next.

고쳐쓰기

틀린 문장을 쓰고 올바르게 고치세요.

______ → ______

● TOSEL 기출문제 변형 수능/내신 출제유형

틀린 문장 고르기

다음 중 문법적으로 틀린 것을 고르세요.

The heaviest cats in the world ① **are** tigers. Male tigers can weigh as much as 320 kilograms, while female tigers weigh less. Female tigers can weigh as little as 120 kilograms and as much as 180 kilograms. Tiger's coats are ② **usually** orange with dark stripes. The stripes can vary in color ③ **for** dark brown to black. A tiger's stripes are much like finger prints in humans. No two tigers have the same set of stripes. In fact, when a tiger is shaved, his fur grows back ④ **with** the same stripes it had before. People ⑤ **generally** believe the reason for a tiger's stripes is to serve as camouflage in the wild.

고쳐쓰기

틀린 문장을 쓰고 올바르게 고치세요.

→ ____________________

Unit Review

배운 내용 스스로 정리해보기

❶ 전치사

전치사에는 ❶ ____, ❷ ____, ❸ ____, ❹ ____, ❺ ____,
❻ ____ 등이 있으며 전치사 뒤에는 ❼ ____ 또는 목적격 대명사 등이 온다.

예시문장 써보기

❶ ____ → ____________________

❷ ____ → ____________________

❸ ____ → ____________________

❹ ____ → ____________________

❺ ____ → ____________________

❻ ____ → ____________________

연습하기

보기에서 빈칸에 공통으로 들어갈 알맞은 전치사를 골라 써넣으세요.

보기	❶ over	❷ at	❸ with	❹ on

❶ There was a lamp hanging ____ the table.
I jumped ____ the wall.

❷ Don't sit ____ the grass. It's wet.
Lisa is going to the cinema ____ Friday evening.

❸ Julia is working ____ her desk.
Do you want me to meet you ____ the airport?

UNIT 04

접속사

개념	단어, 구, 절을 연결하는 말 Your **dog** **and** **cat** are cute.
종류	❶ **등위접속사: 문법상 대등한 관계를 이어주는 접속사** **I am a math teacher but he is an English teacher.** **You have blue eyes and I have black eyes.** ❷ **종속접속사: 종속절을 주절에 이어주는 접속사** He **will be late** **if** he **doesn't get up early.**

UNIT 4 접속사

① 등위접속사

and	She has blue eyes **and** she wears blue glasses. 주어 동사 주어 동사 You can bring a sandwich **and** eat it. 동사 동사
but	I agree with him **but** I cannot help him. 주어 동사 주어 동사
or	You can run **or** walk to school. 동사 동사
for	It was morning, **for** the birds were singing. 주어 동사 주어 동사
yet	It is a strange story, **yet** it is true. 주어 동사 주어 동사
so	He is old, **so** he needs some help from others. 주어 동사 주어 동사 = He needs some help from others **because** he is old. 종속접속사

② 종속접속사

if	I don't care **if** it doesn't rain. 주어 동사 주어 동사 It is not clear **if** she likes him. 주어 동사 주어 동사
as	**As** it was cold last night, I nearly caught a cold. 주어 동사 주어 동사
since	**Since** you look tired, you had better take a rest. 주어 동사 주어 동사

NOTE

Activity

각 단어를 알맞은 접속사 종류와 연결시키세요.

1. for •
2. yet •
3. and •
4. but •
5. as •
6. so •
7. since •
8. if •

• (a) 등위접속사

• (b) 종속접속사

Exercise

Exercise 1

알맞은 접속사를 넣어 두 문장을 하나의 문장으로 연결하세요.

❶ I can't go to the party tonight. My sister had a car accident.
→ I can't go to the party tonight, ______ my sister had a car accident.

❷ It is cold outside. I need to wear a thick coat.
→ ______ it is cold outside, I need to wear a thick coat.

❸ It is a strange story. It is true.
→ It is a strange story, ______ it is true.

❹ You can run to school. You can walk to school.
→ You can run ______ walk to school.

Exercise 2

둘 중 맞는 단어를 고르세요.

❶ How about talking in the kitchen **but / or** living room?

❷ I want to watch the soccer game, **so / but** there was no TV in the dormitory.

❸ I have to save money, **for / so** I have to buy a present for my parents.

❹ It's only the beginning of autumn, **and / yet** it's chilly at night.

❺ It is not I **but / and** he who is to blame.

Exercise 3

알맞은 종속접속사를 이용해 빈칸을 채워 문장을 완성하세요.

❶ 나는 그 목표를 달성할 수 있을지 없을지 확실하지 않다.
I'm not sure ______ I can achieve the goal or not.

❷ 우리의 민박 가족은 우리에게 우리가 간식들을 충분히 먹었는지 물어보았다.
Our host family asked us ______ we had enough snacks.

❸ 오늘이 힘든 날이었기 때문에, 너는 휴식을 취하는 편이 나을 것 같다.
______ today was a tough day, you had better take a rest.

❹ 당신께서 그 일을 맡을 수 있으시다면 제게 말해주세요.
Please tell me ______ you'll take the job.

❺ 내가 품질 좋고 비싼 드레스를 사고 싶기 때문에, 나는 돈을 벌어야한다.
______ I want to buy a fine and expensive dress, I have to earn money.

Sentence Completion

❶ A : Who was at yesterday's meeting?

B : Tom, Elliott, __________ Janice were there. We had discussion over the project.

(A) but
(B) and
(C) yet
(D) for

❷ A : What's wrong with your computer?

B : It keeps freezing, __________ I am taking it to get fixed.

(A) or
(B) as
(C) so
(D) nor

❸ A : What will you do tonight?

B : I will watch a movie __________ I finish my homework.

(A) if
(B) for
(C) but
(D) and

❹ A : What happened to your eyes? They are all red!

B : Yesterday I went to a flower garden. __________ I am allergic to flower pollen, I got red eyes.

(A) if
(B) for
(C) and
(D) since

❺ A : Did you hear the news? Mike won the first prize!

B : I'm not surprised. __________ he tried his best all this summer, he deserves it.

(A) As
(B) For
(C) But
(D) And

❻ **Which one do you prefer, coffee ________ tea?**

(A) or
(B) yet
(C) but
(D) and

❼ **I love him, ________ we can't be together. He has a girlfriend.**

(A) or
(B) for
(C) but
(D) and

❽ **If you want to lose some weight, you can use my gym. It has yoga, pilates, ________ swimming classes.**

(A) or
(B) for
(C) but
(D) and

❾ **________ you have any further questions, feel free to ask me.**

(A) If
(B) As
(C) Since
(D) Because

❿ **________ I didn't get enough sleep last night, I need some coffee to wake up.**

(A) If
(B) As
(C) Yet
(D) For

Error Recognition

● TOSEL 기출문제 변형 수능/내신 출제유형

틀린 문장 고르기

다음 중 문법적으로 틀린 것을 고르세요.

My dream house is huge! I want it to have two levels. There will be four ① **bedrooms** and two bathrooms upstairs. One of the bathrooms will be inside my bedroom. There will be a kitchen, a living room, a dining room, an office, and another bathroom downstairs. My uncle is a carpenter ② **so** he is going to help me build it. He has built many houses. The most important part ③ **of** my dream house is where I build it. I want it to be next to the ocean. ④ **But** I lived by the ocean when I was younger, I really miss it. When I open my bedroom window ⑤ **at** night, I want to hear the waves crashing on the beach. If the air is cool, I will have a fire in my fireplace. I can't wait to build my dream house!

고쳐쓰기

틀린 문장을 쓰고 올바르게 고치세요.

→ ______________________

● TOSEL 기출문제 변형 수능/내신 출제유형

틀린 문장 고르기

다음 중 문법적으로 틀린 것을 고르세요.

Summer in Korea is very hot! People try ① **but** find many ways to stay cool in the summer. One popular way to stay cool is to wear light clothing. Shorts and t-shirts are helpful. But ② **because** that's not enough, many of the modern buildings have air conditioning. An air conditioner is a machine that lowers the temperature of the air, ③ **so** it's a great feeling to walk into an air-conditioned movie theater in the middle of the summer. It makes watching a movie a great way to relax on ④ **hot** days. The most enjoyable way to stay cool ⑤ **is** to have a big ice cream cone! It's cool and delicious.

고쳐쓰기

틀린 문장을 쓰고 올바르게 고치세요.

→ ______________________

Unit Review

배운 내용 스스로 정리해보기

❶ 등위접속사

등위접속사의 종류는 ❶ ______, ❷ ______, ❸ ______, ❹ ______, ❺ ______, ❻ ______ 등이 있다.

예시문장 써보기

❶ ______ → ______

❷ ______ → ______

❸ ______ → ______

❹ ______ → ______

❺ ______ → ______

❻ ______ → ______

❷ 종속접속사

종속접속사의 종류는 ❶ ______, ❷ ______, ❸ ______ 등이 있다.

예시문장 써보기

❶ ______ → ______

❷ ______ → ______

❸ ______ → ______

TOSEL 실전문제 2

PART 6. Sentence Completion

DIRECTIONS: In this portion of the test, you will be given 10 incomplete sentences. From the choices provided, choose the word or words that correctly complete the sentence. Then, fill in the corresponding space on your answer sheet.

1. A: Your coat looks stained.
   B: The waitress spilled a glass of wine on my coat. I will ______ it.

   (A) complain
   (B) complain to
   (C) complain about
   (D) be complaining in

2. A: Where were you yesterday?
   B: I was at Celine's graduation ceremony. She ______ middle school.

   (A) graduates
   (B) graduated
   (C) graduated in
   (D) graduated from

3. A: What time is it now? I lost track of time because of this game.
   B: You must go ______ now, otherwise you'll be late.

   (A) right
   (B) rightly
   (C) rightness
   (D) right away

4. A: Susan, where is your dog?
   B: She just entered ______ the back door of my house by herself.

   (A) of
   (B) at
   (C) on
   (D) through

5. A: Where are your parents today?
   B: They might be at home ______ at the gym.

   (A) or
   (B) and
   (C) but
   (D) since

6. Not only Charles but also I ______ to go shopping at the department store.

(A) like
(B) likes
(C) is liking
(D) am liking

7. He ______ the mechanism of how the semiconductor works during the lecture.

(A) mention
(B) mentioned
(C) mentioned to
(D) mentioned about

8. Increasing awareness of environmental problems has been proved by the statistics ______.

(A) late
(B) later
(C) lately
(D) of late on

9. I was so shocked by the news that our professor died ______ lung cancer.

(A) in
(B) at
(C) on
(D) of

10. ______ Terry didn't obey the rules, he will be punished by the school policy.

(A) If
(B) For
(C) But
(D) Since

Error Recognition

1. 다음 중 문법적으로 틀린 것을 골라 고치세요.

● TOSEL 기출문제 변형 수능/내신 출제유형

1

Daphne was a beautiful water maiden. She was the daughter of the river god Peneus. Everyone loved her, but she didn't want to ❶ **marry with** someone. She wanted to play in the forest with the animals. One day the god Apollo saw her. He fell in love with her ❷ **instantly** . Apollo was strong and handsome, but Daphne did not like him. She ran away from him, and he ❸ **chased** her through the forest.

→ ______________________

2. 다음 밑줄 친 부분을 바르게 고치세요.

● TOSEL 기출문제 변형 수능/내신 출제유형

2

Mr. Dawod is sixty years old, and he lives **<u>at</u>** Jewel Street. Everyone near Jewel Street knows him. Mr. Dawod is really popular. Why is he popular? First, he bakes bread in his kitchen on Mondays. Then, he takes the warm bread to his elderly neighbors. People enjoy his visits because he tells funny stories. Second, Mr. Dawod grows watermelons in summer. He takes the watermelons to families. Finally, Mr. Dawod feeds street cats every day.

→ ______________________

CHAPTER 03

III. 문장의 구조

UNIT 01

문장성분의 기초

종류	주어(S), 동사(V), 목적어(O), 보어(C) **He bought the drawer** yesterday. 주어 동사 목적어
쓰임	❶ **주어(S)**: 동작이나 상태의 주체를 나타냄 **The cat** chased the dog. ❷ **동사(V)**: 동작이나 상태를 나타냄 The cat **chased** the dog. ❸ **목적어(O)**: 동작의 대상을 나타냄 The cat chased **the dog**. ❹ **보어(C)**: 주어와 목적어를 보충함 She became **a venture businessman**.

① 주어(S)

<u>The washing machine</u> is not working.

<u>The movie director</u> should be creative.

<u>I</u> was studying math, so <u>I</u> couldn't answer your call.

② 동사(V)

This <u>is</u> a well-organized room.

Let's <u>watch</u> this movie together tomorrow.

I <u>understand</u> you.

③ 목적어(O)

I really want to buy <u>that ice cream</u> for my cousin.

If you don't mind, I will close <u>the window</u>.

They saw <u>the girl</u> yesterday.

④ 보어(C)

주격보어 When I grow up, I want to be <u>a teacher</u>.

목적격보어 My grandmother calls me <u>piggy</u>.

NOTE

Activity

각 예문에 알맞은 문장 성분을 보기에서 찾아보세요.

보기	❶ 동사	❷ 주어	❸ 목적어	❹ 보어

❶ **I want to buy that ice cream** for my cousin.

❷ **I want to be a scientist** when I grow up.

❸ **I was studying math**.

❹ **My father** always **calls me piggy**.

❺ **He wants to know about which flower she likes**.

❻ **She goes** to school.

❼ **We are very happy** about the competition result.

❽ **I want to raise a dog**.

❾ **The leaves of the trees turned green**.

❿ **I cleaned my room** perfectly.

Exercise

Exercise 1

문장의 주어에 밑줄, 동사에 동그라미를 쳐보세요.

1. The boy **kicked** the ball.
2. He **knows** the truth.
3. The man **sat** on the adjacent sofa.
4. Her daughter **was born** in Chicago.
5. The washing machine **is broken.**

Exercise 2

밑줄 친 부분이 목적어인지 보어인지 구별해보세요.

1. I love **my boyfriend**. **(목적어 / 보어)**
2. They are **students** from France. **(목적어 / 보어)**
3. Tigers are big **animals**. **(목적어 / 보어)**
4. My daughter made **a doll**. **(목적어 / 보어)**
5. The leaves turned **red**. **(목적어 / 보어)**

Exercise 3

밑줄 친 부분의 문장성분을 파악해보세요.

1. **They** **saw** the boy two days ago.

2. **I** will close **the window** since it's too cold outside.

3. This **is** a well-organized **room**.

4. This book **is** **interesting**.

5. **My friends** enjoy **swimming** as a hobby.

Sentence Completion

❶ A : How was the movie last night?

B : The ______ was so good. I loved it.

(A) act
(B) acting
(C) acted
(D) was acting

❷ A : Do you ______ any other opinions about this subject?

B : I think option A seems better.

(A) have
(B) had to
(C) have to
(D) have got to

❸ A : What is your weekend plan?

B : I am going to ______ my grandmother.

(A) so
(B) fun
(C) visit
(D) early

❹ A : I ran into ______ at the park today.

B : Really? How's he doing?

(A) sad
(B) Charles
(C) clumsy
(D) because

❺ A : Your room is so ______ ! You should clean your room right now.

B : Okay, I will.

(A) mess
(B) messy
(C) messily
(D) messing

6 The ________ should be creative and hardworking.

(A) write
(B) writer
(C) writing
(D) written

7 You should totally ________ her right now. She is worrying about you.

(A) call
(B) caller
(C) called
(D) calling

8 Let's go to the mall. I ________ to buy some clothes for the party.

(A) what
(B) want
(C) wait
(D) waist

9 Tomorrow is my mother's birthday. I made a ________ for her.

(A) any
(B) beg
(C) cake
(D) drinking

10 The movie became ________ as I watched. I shouldn't have started it.

(A) horror
(B) horrible
(C) horribly
(D) more horribly

Error Recognition

● TOSEL 기출문제 변형 수능/내신 출제유형

틀린 문장 고르기

다음 중 문법적으로 틀린 것을 고르세요.

I love to travel. The last place I visited ① **was** Washington, DC. It's the capital of America. It's where the president lives. He lives in a house called The White House. I got my photo taken in front of it. My friends thought that it was really ② **neat** . I also got to visit many great museums. ③ **The museums** in DC are called Smithsonian's. They are all free. My mom liked that we didn't have to spend any money. After we visited three museums in one day I was very tired. My mother let ④ **me** buy a hotdog from a man selling from a cart on the street. It was ⑤ **deliciously** .

고쳐쓰기

틀린 문장을 쓰고 올바르게 고치세요.

→ ______________________

● TOSEL 기출문제 변형 수능/내신 출제유형

틀린 문장 고르기

다음 중 문법적으로 틀린 것을 고르세요.

Peggy's Cove is a ① **place** where many tourists visit each summer. It is in Nova Scotia, Canada. Peggy's Cove is the most photographed lighthouse in the world. It is also one of the few lighthouses that is also a post office. People ② **coming** from all over the world to mail letters from the lighthouse. Peggy's Cove is by the ocean. There are huge, flat rocks that let you walk close to the water. The waves are ③ **strong** and often hit the rocks. Tourists are warned not to get too close to the water. Some tourists do not ④ **listen to** the warnings. Every year one or two tourists get too close and are swept out to sea. The sea is rough and cold. The tourists who stay a safe distance from the water ⑤ **are** smart.

고쳐쓰기

틀린 문장을 쓰고 올바르게 고치세요.

→ ____________________

Unit Review

배운 내용 스스로 정리해보기

❶ 주어(S)

주어는 ❶ 동작이나 ❷ 상태의 ______ 을(를) 나타낸다.

예시문장 써보기

______ → ______________________________

❷ 동사(V)

동사는 ❶ ______ 또는 ❷ ______ 를 나타낸다.

예시문장 써보기

❶ ______ 을(를) 나타내는 서술어 → ______________________________

❷ ______ 을(를) 나타내는 서술어 → ______________________________

❸ 목적어(O)

목적어는 동작의 ______ 을(를) 나타낸다.

예시문장 써보기

______ → ______________________________

❹ 보어(C)

보어는 ❶ ______ 와(과) ❷ ______ 을(를) 보충한다.

예시문장 써보기

❶ ______ 을(를) 보충하는 보어 → ______________________________

❷ ______ 을(를) 보충하는 보어 → ______________________________

UNIT 02

문장의 형식

종류	
	❶ **1형식:** 주어 + 완전자동사 (S + V) There **is a park** near my home. ❷ **2형식:** 주어 + 불완전자동사 + 보어 (S + V + S.C) **Jane remained silent.** ❸ **3형식:** 주어 + 타동사 + 목적어(S + V + O) **Nick found a missing doll** for his sister. ❹ **4형식:** 주어 + 완전타동사 + 간접목적어 + 직접목적어 (S + V + I.O + D.O) **He promised me nothing.** ❺ **5형식:** 주어 + 불완전타동사 + 목적어 + 목적격보어 (S + V + O + O.C) **I believe her honest.**

① 1형식 (S+V)

I run.
주어 동사

Chocolate melts.
주어 동사

② 2형식 (S+V+S.C)

That sounds great.
주어 동사 보어

Timmy is a doctor.
주어 동사 보어

③ 3형식 (S+V+O)

He ate a watermelon.
주어 동사 목적어

I learned psychology.
주어 동사 목적어

③ 4형식 (S+V+I.O+D.O)

Mr. Olive gave Mrs. Olive a flower.
주어 동사 간접목적어 직접목적어

= Mr. Olive gave a flower to Mrs. Olive. 3형식
주어 동사 목적어 전치사구

He bought me a watch.
주어 동사 간접목적어 직접목적어

= He bought a watch for me. 3형식
주어 동사 목적어 전치사구

③ 5형식 (S+V+O+O.C)

People call him a national hero.
주어 동사 목적어 목적격 보어

The movie always makes me sad.
주어 동사 목적어 목적격 보어

NOTE

TIP 유도부사 (There, Here)

- There / Here + be동사 + 주어 + 수식어구

→ 1형식으로 분류
→ There / Here은 해석하지 않음.

예문) There are many different kinds of IQ tests.

TIP 수여동사

- 이중목적어를 취하는 동사

give	주다
pay	지불하다
buy	사다(사주다)
promise	약속하다
owe	빚지다

TIP 이중목적어를 취하는 동사

- 4형식 문장을 3형식으로 전환할 때, to/for/of/on/against의 전치사를 취할 수 있음.

Activity

다음 문장을 형식으로 구분해보세요.

1. He gave me a beautiful flower. (   )
2. We remained silent during the show. (   )
3. Trees grow slowly. (   )
4. I heard her singing a song loudly. (   )
5. I especially like this doll. (   )
6. He sent me an email regarding the recruitment. (   )
7. I bought a present for her. (   )
8. My father made me clean my messy room. (   )
9. We found the movie very intriguing. (   )
10. I felt tired after the exercise. (   )

Exercise

Exercise 1

밑줄 친 부분의 문장성분을 S, V, C, I.O, D.O, O.C 로 구분하고 형식을 구분해보세요.

❶ **Her uncle** **gave** **her** **a doll** to play with.

❷ **The chicken soup** **smells** **wonderful**.

❸ **The noise** from outside **keeps** **me** **awake** all night long.

❹ **She** **bought** **me** **a cup of coffee and bagel**.

❺ **The store** **sells** **people** **fresh food**.

Exercise 2

괄호에서 어법상 가장 알맞은 것을 고르세요.

❶ We found her **amuse / amusing** .

❷ Sally is not **guilt / guilty** .

❸ Swimming lets people **maintain / to maintain** their health.

❹ My friend gave some aspirin **for / to** me.

❺ He bought a watch **for / to** me.

Exercise 3

4형식 문장을 3형식으로 바꾸어보세요.

❶ Rachel bought me a brand-new computer.

➡

❷ The curator showed us Monet's early work.

➡

❸ She taught me French words.

➡

❹ He gave me a flower.

➡

❺ He made his girlfriend a handmade cake.

➡

Sentence Completion

❶ A : Where is Carl?

B : He ______ away.

(A) ran
(B) read
(C) made
(D) seemed

❷ A : You ______ especially amazing today.

B : Aww, thank you.

(A) see
(B) look
(C) elect
(D) listen

❸ A : What do you study in college?

B : I study ______ .

(A) economy
(B) economist
(C) economics
(D) economical

❹ A : Look what I got for you! I bought ______ as a birthday present!

B : Thank you so much, mom.

(A) a you bike
(B) bike a you
(C) you a bike
(D) a bike you

❺ A : My classmates elected me ______ !

B : Congratulations!

(A) prevent
(B) prepare
(C) precious
(D) president

❻ **I think I got food poisoning.**

My stomach __________ .

(A) feels
(B) hurts
(C) makes
(D) washes

❼ **Gabriel __________ awesome.**
I wonder what her perfume is.

(A) feels
(B) buys
(C) smells
(D) tastes

❽ **The famous actor signed __________**
for a TV commercial.

(A) hear
(B) bright
(C) continue
(D) a contract

❾ **In 1983, the researchers __________**
Koko some kittens as a birthday present.

(A) spoke
(B) asked
(C) brought
(D) walked

❿ **This swimsuit made the swimmers**
__________ in the water.

(A) light
(B) guess
(C) fitness
(D) athlete

Error Recognition

● TOSEL 기출문제 변형 수능/내신 출제유형

틀린 문장 고르기

다음 중 문법적으로 틀린 것을 고르세요.

How do dolphins breathe? Dolphins must ① **remain** awake to breathe. This means ② **that** they cannot go into a full sleep or they stop breathing. Dolphins are clever animals. They solve this problem by only letting half of their brain sleep at a time. This gives ③ **their** time to rest for up to eight hours a day. Just like people, dolphins are different from each other. They prefer ④ **resting** in different ways. There are three general ways a dolphin can rest. Some dolphins ⑤ **swim** slowly and come to the surface every now and then to breathe. Other dolphins prefer to rest at the surface and leave their blowhole above water. The last way is for dolphins to rest on the bottom, in shallow water, and surface every now and then to breathe.

고쳐쓰기

틀린 문장을 쓰고 올바르게 고치세요.

→ ____________________

● TOSEL 기출문제 변형 수능/내신 출제유형

틀린 문장 고르기

다음 중 문법적으로 틀린 것을 고르세요.

Pac-man ① was a popular video game in the 1980s. It was a big hit for the Atari company. People called ② itself the best game. Atari was one of the most popular video game companies during that time. They made many entertaining games that children and adults both loved. Pac-man was ③ their best seller. The game was very simple. A yellow face ④ raced through a maze to eat white dots while being chased by ghosts. The game was simple compared to today's games, but people loved ⑤ it !

고쳐쓰기

틀린 문장을 쓰고 올바르게 고치세요.

→ ____________________

Unit Review

배운 내용 스스로 정리해보기

문장의 형식

문장의 형식은 5개로 나누어질 수 있다. 1형식은 ❶ ______, 2형식은 ❷ ______, 3형식은 ❸ ______, 4형식은 ❹ ______, 5형식은 ❺ ______ 로 구성된다.

예시문장 써보기

❶ 1형식 ______ → ______

❷ 2형식 ______ → ______

❸ 3형식 ______ → ______

❹ 4형식 ______ → ______

❺ 5형식 ______ → ______

연습하기

밑줄 친 부분에 따라 문장 구성 요소를 알파벳 약어로 써본 후, 몇 형식 문장인지 맞춰보세요.

❶ Sugar tastes sweet. → ___ 형식
S ( ) ( )

❷ He makes me laugh every day. → ___ 형식
S ( ) ( ) ( )

❸ She studied all night to pass the exam. → ___ 형식
( ) ( )

❹ Tom caught a fish with his bare hands. → ___ 형식
( ) ( ) ( )

❺ My friend brought me a lunch box. → ___ 형식
( ) ( ) ( ) ( )

UNIT 03

평서문의 전환

생김새	**4형식 문장의 3형식 문장으로의 전환** 4형식 I gave him a brand new laptop. 3형식 I gave a brand new laptop **to** him.
방법	I sent the professor an email. Step1. **4형식 문장의 간접목적어와 직접목적어 자리 바꾸기** I sent an email the professor. Step2. **간접목적어 앞에 알맞은 전치사 삽입하기** I sent an email **to** the professor.

① 4형식 문장과 3형식 문장의 전환

4형식 I owe Victoria my success.
주어 동사 간접목적어 직접목적어

= 3형식 I owe my success to Victoria.
주어 동사 목적어 전치사구

4형식 I paid him 10 dollars.
주어 동사 간접목적어 직접목적어

= 3형식 I paid 10 dollars to him.
주어 동사 목적어 전치사구

② 문장의 전환과 전치사

❶ to (give, lend, offer, promise, send, teach, write, etc.)

4형식 My friend will teach me algebra.
➜ 3형식 My friend will teach algebra to me.

❷ for (build, buy, choose, cook, find, get, keep, make, etc.)

4형식 She is cooking me ratatouille.
➜ 3형식 She is cooking ratatouille for me.

❸ of (ask, demand, inquire, request, require, etc.)

4형식 He asked me a question.
➜ 3형식 He asked a question of me.

❹ on (play, impose, force, enjoin, urge, etc.)

4형식 They played me a trick.
➜ 3형식 They played a trick on me.

❺ against (bear, etc.)

4형식 I bear you no malice.
➜ 3형식 I bear no malice against you.

NOTE

Activity

다음 문장을 보고 3형식, 4형식을 구분해보세요.

❶ I owe Victoria my success. (3형식/4형식)

❷ My friend will teach algebra to me. (3형식/4형식)

❸ She is cooking me spaghetti. (3형식/4형식)

❹ They played a trick on me. (3형식/4형식)

❺ I bear you no malice. (3형식/4형식)

❻ I will cook lunch for him. (3형식/4형식)

❼ They asked me a difficult question. (3형식/4형식)

❽ Could you please give him these pictures? (3형식/4형식)

❾ She showed me her collection of souvenirs. (3형식/4형식)

❿ He told a lot about the company to new employees. (3형식/4형식)

Exercise

Exercise 1

빈칸을 채워 문장을 완성하세요.

1. He gave some advice ______ me.
2. She bought a gift ______ her younger brother.
3. Jane asked endless questions ______ her older sister.
4. Would you please order a glass of wine ______ me?
5. They offered a decent job ______ her.

Exercise 2

둘 중 맞는 단어를 고르세요.

1. My friend wrote a letter **to / for** me to apologize.
2. She reads a story every night **to / for** her baby.
3. She lent her laptop **to / for** me.
4. I asked a favor **of / for** her to pick up my dress.
5. The mom cooked chicken soup **to / for** her sick child.

Exercise 3

3형식이면 4형식으로, 4형식이면 3형식으로 문장을 바꿔보세요.

❶ My parents bought me a laptop.

➡

❷ I would like to ask Mr.Jones a few questions.

➡

❸ The hotel offered us nice service.

➡

❹ My friend told an interesting story to me.

➡

❺ He made an apple pie for her.

➡

Sentence Completion

❶ A : Why are you smiling?

B : My mother bought a computer ______.

(A) me

(B) my

(C) for me

(D) for myself

❷ A : I owe you ______. I am so sorry.

B : It's okay.

(A) an apology

(B) to an apology

(C) for an apology

(D) with an apology

❸ A : What are you doing now?

B : I am cooking chicken soup ______ my grandfather.

(A) to

(B) of

(C) for

(D) against

❹ A : Can I ask a small favor ______ you?

B : Sure. Anytime.

(A) to

(B) of

(C) for

(D) against

❺ A : Mike, where is the document I gave you yesterday?

B : I sent it ______ assistant manager.

(A) to

(B) of

(C) for

(D) against

6 When I visited Bangkok, the orphan girl gave me ______ .

(A) a flower
(B) to a flower
(C) on a flower
(D) for a flower

7 Katie was mad because her boyfriend told ______ a lie.

(A) she
(B) her
(C) to her
(D) with her

8 Michelangelo made the sculpture ______ the church.

(A) to
(B) on
(C) of
(D) for

9 The new professor will teach statistics 101 ______ freshmen.

(A) to
(B) on
(C) of
(D) for

10 My brother used to play a trick ______ me every time.

(A) to
(B) on
(C) of
(D) for

Error Recognition

● TOSEL 기출문제 변형 수능/내신 출제유형

틀린 문장 고르기

다음 중 문법적으로 틀린 것을 고르세요.

Sue and her mother always go shopping for clothes together. Sue is ① **tall** and her mother is short, so they rarely buy the same clothes. Her mother buys pants that ② **are** too long, so she takes them to a tailor to get mended. She does the same thing ③ **with** skirts. It's harder for Sue to find nice skirts and pants to buy. She can only buy them if they are ④ **exactly** right length. So, her mother can't buy them ⑤ **Sue** too.

고쳐쓰기

틀린 문장을 쓰고 올바르게 고치세요.

→ ____________________

● TOSEL 기출문제 변형 수능/내신 출제유형

틀린 문장 고르기

다음 중 문법적으로 틀린 것을 고르세요.

Popcorn is a healthy snack. It is healthier than potato chips or candy. The reason popcorn isn't always good for you ❶ **is** because of the extra toppings people add. The most popular topping to put ❷ **on** popcorn is butter. Butter makes popcorn less healthy because it gives extra fat ❸ **of popcorn**. Popcorn ❹ **and** butter are a delicious treat but it is not something to eat every day! Popcorn is not only ❺ **healthy**, but also easy to cook. It only takes five minutes in the microwave for a fresh, hot snack.

고쳐쓰기

틀린 문장을 쓰고 올바르게 고치세요.

→ ______________________

Unit Review

배운 내용 스스로 정리해보기

❶ 4형식 문장과 3형식 문장의 전환

❶ ______ 문장을 ❷ ______ 문장으로 전환할 수 있다.

예시문장 써보기

❶ lend가 동사인 4형식 → ______________________

❷ 위 문장을 3형식으로 전환 → ______________________

❷ 문장의 전환과 전치사

삽입되는 전치사의 종류에는 ❶ ______, ❷ ______, ❸ ______, ❹ on, ❺ against가 있다.

예시문장 써보기

❶ ______ 을(를) 취하는 동사가 사용된 4형식 → ______________________

위 문장을 3형식으로 전환 → ______________________

❷ ______ 을(를) 취하는 동사가 사용된 4형식 → ______________________

위 문장을 3형식으로 전환 → ______________________

❸ ______ 을(를) 취하는 동사가 사용된 4형식 → ______________________

위 문장을 3형식으로 전환 → ______________________

UNIT 04

의문문의 비교

종류	
종류	❶ **의문사가 있는 의문문**: '의문사 + be동사 + 주어 ~?', '의문사 + 조동사 + 주어 + 동사원형 ~?' 형태이며, Yes/No로 대답 불가능 **What is your plan?** ❷ **의문사가 없는 의문문**: 'Be동사 + 주어 ~?', 'Do + 주어 + 동사원형 ~?' 형태이며, Yes/No로 대답 가능 **Do you speak German?** ❸ **조동사 의문문**: '조동사 + 주어 + 동사원형 ~?' 형태이며, Yes/No로 대답 가능 **Can I play tennis now?** ❹ **부가의문문**: 평서문 뒤에 덧붙이는 의문문으로, 긍정문 뒤에는 부정, 부정문 뒤에는 긍정으로 쓰며, Yes/No로 대답 가능 **She was busy, wasn't she?**

의문문의 비교

① 의문문의 종류

일반의문	Q. Do you speak English? A. Yes, I do.
선택의문	Q. Which do you like better, coffee or tea? A. I like coffee better.
부정의문	Q. Aren't you a doctor? A. No, I am not.
부가의문	Q. It's very hot, isn't it? A. Yes, it is.
수사의문	Q. Who can solve it? = No one can solve it.
간접의문	Q. Do you know when(의문사) he(주어) will(조동사) come(동사원형)? A. No, I'm not sure when he will come.

② 직접의문문과 간접의문문

직접의문문 Who(의문사) is(be동사) the winner(주어)?
= 간접의문문 Do you know who(의문사) the winner(주어) is(be동사)?

직접의문문 Where(의문사) is(be동사) Isabel(주어) going?
= 간접의문문 Do you know where(의문사) Isabel(주어) is(be동사) going?

Q. 직접의문문 What(의문사) is(be동사) this(주어)?

A. 간접의문문 I also don't know what(의문사) this(주어) is(be동사).

NOTE

Activity

각 문장을 알맞은 의문문의 종류로 구별해보세요.

보기 ① 부가의문 ② 수사의문 ③ 간접의문 ④ 일반의문 ⑤ 선택의문 ⑥ 부정의문

① Do you speak English? ( )

② Aren't you a doctor? ( )

③ Who can solve it? ( )

④ Do you know when he will come? ( )

⑤ It's very cold, isn't it? ( )

⑥ She didn't turn off the light, did she? ( )

⑦ Do you know how he solved this difficult puzzle? ( )

⑧ Don't you think so? ( )

⑨ Do you have extra money to pay the city tax? ( )

⑩ He is going to the swimming pool, isn't he? ( )

Exercise

Exercise 1

각 문장을 주어진 의문문으로 바꾸어보세요.

1. She is sleepy. (부가의문문)
→ ______
2. You can't dance. (부가의문문)
→ ______
3. He was absent. (부가의문문)
→ ______
4. The food tasted good. (일반의문문)
→ ______

Exercise 2

빈칸을 채워 의문문을 완성해보세요.

1. Jake plays badminton every Sunday.
→ ______ Jake ______ badminton every Sunday?
2. She answered her daughter's question.
→ ______ she ______ her daughter's question?
3. The book was boring.
→ ______ the book boring?
4. They are good neighbors.
→ ______ they good neighbors?

Exercise 3

두 문장을 연결해서 간접 의문문으로 만들어 보세요.

❶ Do you know? Where are our gifts?

➡

❷ Do you know? What time does the class start?

➡

❸ Can you tell me? How much is this camera?

➡

❹ Do you know? What color did she choose for the banner?

➡

❺ Do you understand? What does she mean?

➡

Sentence Completion

❶ A : ________ do you like more, purple or pink?
B : I like purple more.

(A) Who
(B) What
(C) Which
(D) Where

❷ A : This bag seems nice, ________ ?
B : Yeah, it's cute. You should buy one.

(A) is it
(B) isn't it
(C) are they
(D) aren't they

❸ A : Do you know where ________ ?
B : I don't know. Ask Shelly.

(A) Mike lives
(B) lives Mike
(C) does Mike live
(D) does live Mike

❹ A : Can you tell me why ________ ?
B : I heard that she is sick.

(A) absent is Sooyoung
(B) is Sooyoung absent
(C) is absent Sooyoung
(D) Sooyoung is absent

❺ A : I wonder when ________ .
B : He will come back in January.

(A) will he come back
(B) will come he back
(C) he will come back
(D) he come will back

6 **This problem is too hard to solve. Who ______ it?**

(A) can solve
(B) solve can
(C) does can solve
(D) can does solve

7 **Elisa called me and cried for almost two hours. She is too emotional, ______ ?**

(A) is she
(B) does she
(C) isn't she
(D) doesn't she

8 **Can you tell me where the nearest ______ ?**

(A) is station
(B) station is
(C) does station
(D) station does

9 **I'd like to know where ______ yesterday.**

(A) went you
(B) you went
(C) did you go
(D) did go you

10 **Can you remember who ______ the wallet?**

(A) stole
(B) stolen
(C) did steal
(D) didn't steal

Error Recognition

● TOSEL 기출문제 변형 수능/내신 출제유형

틀린 문장 고르기

다음 중 문법적으로 틀린 것을 고르세요.

Kristy is looking for a new hobby. She has already tried many different things. She joined a soccer team, but she didn't like to run. Running ① **is** an important part of soccer. Next she tried ballet. She kept falling over her feet. ② **Being graceful** is an important part of ballet. Next she tried swimming, but she didn't like being wet. Finally she tried taking photos. She loved it! She could take photos of all her friends and family. ③ **When** she printed out her photos, she made beautiful albums ④ **for** everyone. Kristy finally found her perfect hobby! ⑤ **Which** knew that she likes to take photos?

고쳐쓰기

틀린 문장을 쓰고 올바르게 고치세요.

→ ______________________

● TOSEL 기출문제 변형 수능/내신 출제유형

틀린 문장 고르기

다음 중 문법적으로 틀린 것을 고르세요.

Monica's family went camping last week. Her family ① **really** enjoys camping. She usually goes camping with her family while she doesn't know where ② **go they**. They brought two tents to sleep in. Her parents slept ③ **in** the big tent. She slept in the small tent ④ **with** her brother. In the morning, Monica read a book after breakfast. In the afternoon, she went swimming with her brother. In the evening, her dad made a fire. When the fire was ready, the family cooked dinner. After dinner, the family sang songs by the fire ⑤ **and** then went to bed.

고쳐쓰기

틀린 문장을 쓰고 올바르게 고치세요.

→ ________________

Unit Review

배운 내용 스스로 정리해보기

❶ 의문문의 종류

의문문의 종류에는 ❶ 일반의문문, ❷ ______ 의문문, ❸ 부정의문문, ❹ ______ 의문문, ❺ 수사의문문, ❻ ______ 의문문이 있다.

예시문장 써보기

❶ ______ 의문문 → ______________________

❷ ______ 의문문 → ______________________

❸ ______ 의문문 → ______________________

❷ 직접의문문과 간접의문문

직접의문문은 '(의문사) + (조)동사 + 주어 ~'의 어순으로 나타나는 반면,

간접의문문은 다른 절에 종속되어 ______________________ 의 어순으로 나타난다.

예시문장 써보기

의문사로 시작하는 직접의문문 → ______________________

위 문장을 간접의문문으로 변형 → ______________________

TOSEL 실전문제 ③

PART 6. Sentence Completion

DIRECTIONS: In this portion of the test, you will be given 10 incomplete sentences. From the choices provided, choose the word or words that correctly complete the sentence. Then, fill in the corresponding space on your answer sheet.

1. A: You look happy. What happened?
B: I got ______ from my mother.

(A) a present
(B) presented
(C) presenting
(D) having presentation

2. A: Why the long face?
B: I got below average score. The exam was too ______.

(A) ease
(B) difficult
(C) difficulty
(D) easiness

3. A: Oh, your new computer looks nice.
B: Of course. My dad bought ______ this computer.

(A) me
(B) to me
(C) for me
(D) myself

4. A: Do I need to bring a bluetooth speaker to the picnic?
B: You don't have to, because Sally will bring it ______ us.

(A) of
(B) to
(C) for
(D) about

5. A: Do you understand what ______?
B: Not at all. I will ask questions to her after the lecture.

(A) is she try say
(B) she trying to say
(C) is she trying to say
(D) she is trying to say

6. The doctor always ______ kids a candy after the treatment.

(A) gift
(B) gives
(C) giver
(D) given

7. After she moved to a new house, she painted her bedroom ______.

(A) color
(B) brush
(C) lovely
(D) purple

8. Gabriel made ______ a handmade wooden table for my birthday.

(A) my
(B) me
(C) to me
(D) for me

9. He always checks if everything is in place. He is too meticulous, ______?

(A) is he
(B) do he
(C) isn't he
(D) doesn't he

10. He wants to know how much ______. He is living on a tight budget.

(A) it will cost
(B) will it cost
(C) does it cost
(D) costly it does

Error Recognition

1. 다음 중 문법적으로 틀린 것을 골라 고치세요.

● TOSEL 기출문제 변형 수능/내신 출제유형

1

If you're looking for an easy and delicious treat, ❶ **trying** this simple spinach dip. Mix one package of frozen spinach with one package of cream cheese. Melt ❷ **it** together and add one spoon chili powder. Finally, add ❸ **one cup of milk** and serve with chips or crackers. Your friends will love it!

➔ ____________________

2. 다음 밑줄 친 부분을 바르게 고치세요.

● TOSEL 기출문제 변형 수능/내신 출제유형

2

Nowadays, armies fight with each other from a distance far away with missiles and airplanes, but this is not a new idea. More than 700 years ago, the Chinese army was doing the same thing, only with birds. They would tie hot rocks around the necks of birds and send them **for** enemies. The birds were difficult to control, however, and the Chinese army started using paper rockets. This was centuries before missiles became common in war.

→ ____________________

Answers

Short Answers

CHAPTER 1

p.20

UNIT 1 p.23

Activity

1. (b) 2. (d) 3. (b) 4. (a) 5. (c) 6. (c) 7. (e) 8. (a) 9. (d) 10. (e)

Exercise 1 p.24

1. candles 2. cheese 3. revolves 4. are 5. care

Exercise 2

1. computers 2. fantasy 3. has 4. were 5. The employed

Exercise 3

1. are 2. goes 3. gold 4. many 5. are 6. injured

Sentence Completion p.26

1. (B) 2. (D) 3. (B) 4. (D) 5. (D) 6. (C) 7. (A) 8. (C) 9. (D) 10. (D)

Error Recognition p.28

1. (4) coexists → coexist 2. (3) find → finds

Unit Review p.30

1. ❶ 가산명사 ❷ 불가산명사
➔ I put her keys on the desk yesterday. ➔ He was blamed for leaking information to the company.

2. ❶ 집합명사 ❷ 군집명사
➔ Jimmy's family is a large one. ➔ Her family were divided in their opinions.

3. ❶ The youth should respect the old. ❷ The deceased left much money to his son.
❸ There are two reasons why this is the true.

UNIT 2 p.33

Activity

1. (d) 2. (c) 3. (a), (c) 4. (b) 5. (e) 6. (b) 7. (e) (8) (d) (9) (c) (10) (a)

Exercise 1 p.34

1. her granddaughter a present 2. has to read them
3. painting the wall by himself 4. other flowers are yellow

Exercise 2

1. myself 2. it 3. his 4. We 5. the other

Exercise 3

1. my 2. themselves 3. mine
4. us 5. another 6. both

Sentence Completion p.36

1. (C) 2. (A) 3. (C) 4. (D) 5. (C) 6. (B) 7. (C) 8. (A) 9. (C) 10. (D)

Error Recognition p.38

1. (2) mine → me 2. (2) us → our

Unit Review p.40

1. ❶ his ❷ her ❸ us ❹ yourselves ❺ their
❶ She borrowed his pencil. ❷ He couldn't persuade her.
❸ us ➔ She protected us from danger.

2. ❶ 부정대명사
❶ One / The other ❷ Some / others

UNIT 3 p.43

Activity

1. 전치수식 2. 후치수식 3. 후치수식 4. 전치수식 5. 한정적 용법 6. 한정적 용법 7. 서술적 용법

Exercise 1 p.44

1. (A) dangerous 2. (A) little 3. (A) many 4. (B) mad

Exercise 2

1. lonely 2. being 3. much 4. many 5. enjoyable

Exercise 3

1. challenging 2. strange 3. anything
4. Lots of(A lot of) 5. interesting 6. powerful

Sentence Completion p.46

1. (C) 2. (A) 3. (D) 4. (B) 5. (B) 6. (C) 7. (C) 8. (C) 9. (D) 10. (D)

Error Recognition p.48

1. (2) perfectly → perfect 2. (5) smallest → smaller

Unit Review p.50

1. ① 한정적 용법
   - ① 한정적 용법 ➔ He borrowed my small bag.
2. ① 전치수식 ② 후치수식
   - ① 전치수식 ➔ She bought such a beautiful skirt.
   - ② 후치수식 ➔ John interviewed the actor famous for his voice.
3. ① 셀 수 있는 명사인지 ② 수량형용사의 의미
   - ① Few people attended the class. ② A few people attended the class.
   - ③ We have little money. ④ We have a little money.

UNIT 4 p.53

Activity

1. o 2. x 3. o 4. o 5. x 6. o 7. o 8. x 9. o 10. x

Exercise 1 p.54

1. What a brilliant idea it is! 2. How lucky she is! 3. What a kind boy he is! 4. Wow, that sounds great! 5. What a clever dog he is!

Exercise 2

1. What 2. Ouch 3. What 4. Oops 5. How

Exercise 3

1. How beautiful this flower is! 2. What a smart girl she is! 3. What an interesting question it is! 4. How sad he was! 5. What an amazing place it is!

Sentence Completion p.56

1. (B) 2. (C) 3. (A) 4. (B) 5. (A) 6. (A) 7. (C) 8. (C) 9. (D) 10. (A)

Error Recognition p.58

1. (5) How → What 2. (5) variously → various

Unit Review p.60

1. ① 감탄사
   - ① 감탄사 ➔ Well, I need to go now.
2. ① How ② What ③ 느낌표
   - ① How generous he is! ② What a generous man he is!

TOSEL 실전문제 1 p.61

1. (B) 2. (A) 3. (B) 4. (D) 5. (B) 6. (C) 7. (A) 8. (A) 9. (D) 10. (C)

1. (3) she → her 2. Two tigers no → No two tigers

CHAPTER 2 p.66

UNIT 1 p.69

Activity

1. (a) 2. (a) 3. (b) 4. (a) 5. (b) 6. (a) 7. (b) 8. (b) 9. (b) 10. (b)

Exercise 1 p.70

1. for 2. ø 3. to 4. ø 5. with

Exercise 2

1. ø 2. on 3. for 4. ø 5. ø

Exercise 3

1. work 2. am 3. enjoy 4. is 5. is 6. suffer

Sentence Completion p.72

1. (B) 2. (C) 3. (D) 4. (A) 5. (B) 6. (B) 7. (A) 8. (B) 9. (A) 10. (A)

Error Recognition p.74

1. (4) graduating → graduating from 2. (4) left from → left

Unit Review p.76

1. ① 자동사 ② 타동사
   - ① 자동사 ➔ They live in a small village. ② 타동사 ➔ Lisa admitted her fault.
2. ① I can't wait for my birthday. ② He resembles his mother.
3. ① Not only he but (also) I am good at speaking English.
   - ② Neither I nor Beth was there.

UNIT 2 p.79

Activity

1. (a) 2. (b) 3. (b) 4. (b) 5. (a) 6. (a) 7. (b) 8. (a) 9. (a) 10. (a)

Exercise 1 p.80

1. The world changes rapidly. 2. My children are playing happily.
3. She could find the answer easily. 4. She performed beautifully on the ice rink.

Exercise 2

1. hard 2. lately 3. high 4. freely

Exercise 3

1. 부사, 형용사 2. 부사, 형용사 3. 형용사, 부사 4. 형용사, 부사 5. 부사, 형용사

Sentence Completion p.82

1. (B) 2. (B) 3. (A) 4. (A) 5. (A) 6. (B) 7. (A) 8. (D) 9. (B) 10. (C)

Error Recognition p.84

1. (4) easy → easily 2. (3) free → freely

Unit Review p.86

1. ❶ ly
❶ The world changes rapidly. ❷ My children are playing happily.

2. → My father gets up early. → The early bird catches the worm.

3. ❶ He worked hard all day long. ❷ I can hardly afford to pay the bill.

UNIT 3 p.89

Activity

1. at 2. on 3. in 4. on 5. to 6. with 7. by 8. at

Exercise 1 p.90

1. to 2. at 3. of 4. with

Exercise 2

1. I am very fond of drinking coffee. 2. I was satisfied with the test result.
3. My sister is married to a famous actor. 4. Surprisingly, she specializes in mechanical engineering.

Exercise 3

1. by 2. about 3. of 4. to 5. for

Sentence Completion p.92

1. (B) 2. (C) 3. (D) 4. (A) 5. (C) 6. (A) 7. (B) 8. (C) 9. (A) 10. (D)

Error Recognition p.94

1. (1) at → of 2. (3) for → from

Unit Review p.96

1. ❶ to ❷ on ❸ in ❹ at ❺ of ❻ with ❼ 명사
❶ to → Sally went to the movie theater. ❷ on → Your book is on my desk.
❸ in → I met him in the restaurant. ❹ at → They are waiting for us at their school.
❺ of → The chair is made of wood. ❻ with → I traveled with my grandmother.

2. ❶ over ❷ on ❸ at

UNIT 4 p.99

Activity

1. (a) 2. (a) 3. (a) 4. (a) 5. (b) 6. (a) 7. (b) 8. (b)

Exercise 1 p.100

1. for 2. As / Since 3. yet / but 4. or

Exercise 2

1. or 2. but 3. for 4. yet 5. but

Exercise 3

1. if 2. if 3. As / Since 4. if 5. As / Since

Sentence Completion p.102

1. (B) 2. (C) 3. (A) 4. (D) 5. (A) 6. (A) 7. (C) 8. (D) 9. (A) 10. (B)

Error Recognition p.104

1. (4) But → As 또는 Since 2. (1) but → and

Unit Review p.106

1. ❶ and ❷ but ❸ or ❹ for ❺ yet ❻ so
❶ and / The woman sang a song by day and by night. ❷ but / The pizza is tasty but expensive. ❸ or / You can choose tea or coffee.
❹ for / I was tired, for I studied all night long. ❺ yet / She is small, yet she looks tall. ❻ so / I won the first prize, so I was happy.

2. ❶ if ❷ as ❸ since
❶ if → If you come home early, please clean your room.
❷ as → As he lost his wallet, he couldn't take the subway.
❸ since → She stayed at home since it was raining outside.

TOSEL 실전문제 2 p.107

1. (C) 2. (D) 3. (A) 4. (D) 5. (A) 6. (A) 7. (B) 8. (C) 9. (D) 10. (D)

1. (1) marry with → marry 2. at → on

CHAPTER 3 p.112

UNIT 1 p.115

Activity

1. 2, 1, 3 2. 2, 1, 4 3. 2, 1, 3 4. 2, 1, 3, 4 5. 2, 1, 3 6. 2, 1 7. 2, 1, 4 8. 2, 1, 3 9. 2, 1, 4 10. 2, 1, 3

Exercise 1 p.116

1. 주어 - The boy / 동사 - kicked 2. 주어 - He / 동사 - knows
3. 주어 - The man / 동사 - sat 4. 주어 - Her daughter / 동사 - was born
5. 주어 - The washing machine / 동사 - is broken

Exercise 2

1. 목적어 2. 보어 3. 보어 4. 목적어 5. 보어

Exercise 3

1. They - S(주어) / saw - V(동사) 2. I - S(주어) / the window - O(목적어)
3. is - V(동사) / room - C(보어) 4. is - V(동사) / interesting - C(보어)
5. My friends - S(주어) / swimming - O(목적어)

Sentence Completion p.118	1. (B) 2. (A) 3. (C) 4. (B) 5. (B) 6. (B) 7. (A) 8. (B) 9. (C) 10. (B)
Error Recognition p.120	1. (5) deliciously → delicious 2. (2) coming → come
Unit Review p.122	1. ❷ 주체 ❷ 주체 ➔ Her daughter lives in Chicago. 2. ❶ 동작 ❷ 상태 ❶ 동작 ➔ The boy kicked the ball. ❷ 상태 ➔ He knows the truth. 3. ❶ 대상 ❶ 대상 ➔ Someone broke the window. 4. ❶ 주어 ❷ 목적어 ❶ 주어 ➔ The students grew tired. ❷ 목적어 ➔ She encourages me to participate in a discussion.
UNIT 2 p.125 Activity	1. 4형식 2. 2형식 3. 1형식 4. 5형식 5. 3형식 6. 4형식 7. 3형식 8. 5형식 9. 5형식 10. 2형식
Exercise 1 p.126	1. Her uncle - S, gave - V, her - I.O, doll - D.O / 4형식 2. The chicken soup - S, smells - V, wonderful - C / 2형식 3. The noise - S, keeps - V, me - O, awake - O.C / 5형식 4. She - S, bought - V, me - I.O, a cup of coffee and bagel - D.O / 4형식 5. The store - S, sells - V, people - I.O, fresh food - D.O / 4형식
Exercise 2	1. amusing 2. guilty 3. maintain 4. to 5. for
Exercise 3	1. Rachel bought a brand-new computer for me. 2. The curator showed Monet's early work to us. 3. She taught French words to me. 4. He gave a flower to me. 5. He made a handmade cake for his girlfriend.
Sentence Completion p.128	1. (A) 2. (B) 3. (C) 4. (C) 5. (D) 6. (B) 7. (C) 8. (D) 9. (C) 10. (A)
Error Recognition p.130	1. (3) their → them 2. (2) itself → it
Unit Review p.132	❶ S + V ❷ S + V + C(S.C) ❸ S + V + O ❹ S + V + I.O + D.O ❺ S + V + O + O.C ❶ S + V ➔ They came early in the morning. ❷ S + V + C(S.C) ➔ It seems strange. ❸ S + V + O ➔ He mentioned the subject all day long. ❹ S + V + I.O + D.O ➔ She offered me some advice. ❺ S + V + O + O.C ➔ My mother made me clean my room. ❶ tastes - V, sweet - C → 2 ❷ makes - V, me - O, laugh - C → 5 ❸ She - S, studied - V → 1 ❹ Tom - S, caught - V, a fish - O → 3 ❺ My friend - S, brought - V, me - I.O, a lunch box - D.O → 4
UNIT 3 p.135 Activity	1. 4형식 2. 3형식 3. 4형식 4. 3형식 5. 4형식 6. 3형식 7. 4형식 8. 4형식 9. 4형식 10. 3형식
Exercise 1 p.136	1. to 2. for 3. of 4. for 5. to
Exercise 2	1. to 2. to 3. to 4. of 5. for
Exercise 3	1. My parents bought a laptop for me. 2. I would like to ask a few questions of Mr. Jones. 3. The hotel offered nice service to us. 4. My friend told me an interesting story. 5. He made a her an apple pie.
Sentence Completion p.138	1. (C) 2. (A) 3. (C) 4. (B) 5. (A) 6. (A) 7. (B) 8. (D) 9. (A) 10. (B)
Error Recognition p.140	1. (5) Sue → for Sue 2. (3) of popcorn → to popcorn

Unit Review p.142

1. ❶ 4형식 ❷ 3형식

❶ He lent me his backpack. ❷ He lent his backpack to me.

2. ❶ to ❷ for ❸ of

❶ to → I will show you my work. → I will show my work to you.

❷ for → He made her an apple pie. → He made an apple pie for her.

❸ of → The police asked us a few questions. → The police asked a few questions of us.

UNIT 4 p.145

Activity

1. 일반의문 2. 부정의문 3. 수사의문 4. 간접의문 5. 부가의문 6. 부가의문 7. 간접의문 8. 부정의문 9. 일반의문 10. 부가의문

Exercise 1 p.146

1. She is sleepy, isn't she? 2. You can't dance, can you?

3. He was absent, wasn't he? 4. Did the food taste good?

Exercise 2

1. Does, play 2. Did, answer 3. Was 4. Are

Exercise 3

1. Do you know where our gifts are? 2. Do you know what time the class starts?

3. Can you tell me how much this camera is? 4. Do you know what color she chose for the banner?

5. Do you understand what she means?

Sentence Completion p.148

1. (C) 2. (B) 3. (A) 4. (D) 5. (C) 6. (A) 7. (C) 8. (B) 9. (B) 10. (A)

Error Recognition p.150

1. (5) Which → Who 2. (2) go they → they go

Unit Review p.152

1. ❶ 선택 ❹ 부가 ❻ 간접

❶ 선택 → Do you go to work by car or by subway?

❷ 부가 → We met before, didn't we?

❸ 간접 → Do you know when he will come?

2. ❶ 의문사 / if[whether] + 주어 + 동사~

→ Where is the supermarket? → Could you tell me where the supermarket is?

TOSEL 실전문제 3 p.153

1. (A) 2. (B) 3. (A) 4. (C) 5. (D) 6. (B) 7. (D) 8. (B) 9. (C) 10. (A)

1. (1) trying → try 2. for → to

MEMO